BROKEN
into
WHOLENESS

BOOK OF PEARLS

PEARLENE FRIDAY

I have tried to recreate events, locales, and conversations from my memories of them. In order to maintain their anonymity in some instances, I have changed the names of individuals and places. I may have changed some identifying characteristics and details such as physical properties, occupations, and places of residence.

For permission requests, write to the publisher, addressed:
Jacinth Media Productions
52 N. 2nd Street
Coplay, PA 18037

All Scripture quotes are taken from the Holy Bible, King James Version, Cambridge, NIV 1769; and Bible (The Holy Bible, English Standard Version®) Text Edition: 2016. Copyright © 2001 by Crossway, A publishing ministry of Good News Publishers.

Library of Congress Control Number: 2023912484
ISBN-13: 978-1-960594-12-9 (Paperback)
ISBN-13: 978-1-960594-11-2 (Hardback)
ISBN-13: 978-1-960594-13-6 (E-Book)
This book was printed in the United States

First Printing
10 9 8 7 6 5 4 3 2 1
Book cover design by Jacinth Media Productions

God's Precious Pearls Ministry

Table of Content

Foreword

Sister Pearlene and I met over 38 years ago when we were both young mothers in Richmond, Virginia. She has always expressed her desire to mentor, encourage, and empower women from a Christian perspective. Sister Pearlene is the Founder of God's Precious Pearls (GPP), a ministry for women all over the United States of America who meet biweekly with her, as the leader, for Bible study, prayers, sharing, and encouragement via the phone.

Not until I read the book *Broken Into Wholeness* did I fully understand that she herself had been so deeply hurt in a marriage relationship. She had been so busy helping others that she had not revealed her own pain. In her book, she reveals a willingness to be vulnerable and shares the pain caused by betrayal and a failed marriage.

The book goes on to show how she overcame it. During her own season of brokenness, she had to start over, call on God, and be willing to obey and follow His guidance. Through this obedience, she was brought to wholeness. This is a real-life example of God's grace and our hope in crisis. This author has lived it. The book addresses issues that many who are in failed and failing marriages and relationships are too embarrassed and reluctant to share or seek help. The book takes the reader on a journey with the author from the early days of hopelessness, the dissolution of her marriage, and the challenges of not knowing which way to turn, to providing concrete steps for readers to follow, with self-reflecting questions, scripture references, and prayers.

Broken Into Wholeness targets single, married, and divorced people. It offers solid steps to making the best choices in a partner for those not yet married, building a stronger Christ-centered relationship for marriage and hope for those whose marriages have ended. Sister Pearlene provides her readers with a perfect example of what it looks like to overcome as well as a reminder that we are not alone.

The God we serve is *REAL*.

Venise M. Harrison,
Intercessor
God's Precious Pearls Ministry

Dedication

This book, *Broken into Wholeness*, is dedicated to the most precious people in my life who have been my inspiration and support throughout this journey. To my wonderful daughter, Stephanie, whose unwavering love and belief in me have propelled me forward. My blessed sons Christopher, Nicholas, and Jonathan. To my darling granddaughters, Veda and Josi, and my precious grandsons, Joshua, Thomas, Benjamin, and Fitzgerald, who bring immense joy and remind me of the beauty in life. And to my precious daughters-in-law, whose presence in our family has enriched our lives beyond measure.

You have all ignited a flame within me, urging me to write and share my experiences, in the hope that this book serves as a guiding light for you. As long as the Lord keeps us here on this earth, may it be a road map that leads you towards a blessed, prosperous, and successful life in Him. May every aspect of your lives be embraced by His love, and may His divine direction and guidance be ever-present. May you trust in His choices for you, knowing that they surpass any of your own desires. May your path be filled with clarity, and may you be guided by His everlasting peace.

I pray that the Lord's favor rests upon each of you abundantly, as you wholeheartedly put your trust in Him. Remember the words of Proverbs 3:5-6 (KJV)... *Trust in the Lord with all thine heart; and lean not unto thine own understanding. In all thy ways acknowledge Him and*

He shall direct thy paths.

To my late parents, Deacon Evan Jackson and Deaconess Vielyn Jackson, who faithfully served the Lord and instilled in me the fear and admonition of Him. Your unwavering faith and prayers have been a constant source of strength. Your presence and support have been instrumental in shaping my journey. I am forever grateful for your role as my prayer warriors, especially during the challenges I faced. Without a shadow of a doubt, I know your prayers saved my life.

To my beloved husband, Tom, I express my deepest appreciation for your patience, love, and unwavering encouragement throughout the time I dedicated to completing this book. Your belief in me has been my constant source of motivation and push to keep going.

Special thanks are also due to my sisters and prayer partners of God's Precious Pearls Ministry, whose love and prayers have been a source of strength and inspiration. Your prayers, love, and faith in my abilities have been invaluable. Thank you for trusting me to be your spiritual mother and sister-friend.

Finally, I extend my heartfelt gratitude to everyone who has encouraged me, prayed for me, and offered a listening ear. Your support has meant the world to me, and I cannot thank you enough for being there every step of the way.

Introduction

It has taken me a long time to finally respond to the call to write this book, which has been in the making, but to be honest, I do believe this is indeed God's timing.

During this critical time of the global Covid pandemic, there has been a drastic increase in various abuses within the home. Marriages have been falling apart as husbands and wives struggle to adjust to spending more time together while also working from home. The ability to obtain help has not been readily available, and little or no spiritual food and guidance has been available due to the "lock down" and the inability to attend worship services to fellowship with the saints. As families spent time together, there were clashes in personalities, which was demonstrated in verbal, emotional, and physical abuse.

Never have we witnessed so many broken marriages and wounded hearts as we have in the past two years. During that time, within only about one week, the Lord brought four wonderful women into my life with similar stories of brokenness, pain, and disappointments in their marriages. I knew without any doubt that this was the time to share my testimony of God's love, protection, healing, hope, and restoration. It is important that I answer this call to share our Heavenly Father's guidance and healing so that you too will experience His mighty presence, healing power, and deliverance. We are encouraged that it is God who comforts us in all our troubles, and we are to comfort each other with the comfort that we too have received from Him. (*See 2 Corinthians 1:4*)

This makes one very vulnerable as we share from the very depths of our souls, but I must not forget that our Lord died disgracefully and suffered much for me so that I could be completely delivered and have eternal life with Him. His love certainly has set me free and given me such peace within: "Looking unto Jesus, the author and finisher of our faith; Who for the joy that was set before Him endured the cross, despising the shame, and is set down at the right hand of the throne of God." (*Hebrews 12:2 KJV*)

This book not only talks about God's marvelous healing and restoration, but I want my readers to be aware of the fact that we serve a Mighty God who works in ways that are beyond our understanding. His supernatural intervention in every area of my life even during a time when I encountered a marriage that was very painful and abusive in every way one can possibly think, (infidelity, verbal, physical, sexual, mental, and financial). God intervened as a loving and caring Father in every area. He led, guided, instructed, provided, and closed and opened doors that seemed impossible. He also brought me great comfort, healing, and restoration. He brought wonderful and supportive friends into my life who became family to me: "God sets the solitary in families; He brings out those who are bound into prosperity; but the rebellious dwell in a dry land." (*Psalm 68:6 KJV*)

When we experience emotional pain, there is much more

internal damage that we can neither imagine, nor can we see it in the natural; it is all spiritual. These often lead to various health issues which can include physical and mental illnesses. For every tear we shed, there is a tearing and wounding in our souls, and spiritual bleeding takes place. This does not only lead to physical illnesses but also malignant diseases and subsequent death. Every harsh word spoken to us is an evil arrow and this also causes wounding of our souls. It tears us to the core within.

We give thanks to the Lord for His promises that "The Lord is nigh unto them that are of a broken heart, and saveth such as be of a contrite spirit." (*Psalm 34:18, KJV*)

Scripture also tells us that, "The spirit of a man will sustain his infirmity, but a wounded spirit who can bear?" (*Proverbs 18:14 KJV*). These types of abuses can cause us to lose sight of who we are. It demoralizes us and robs us of our identity, purpose, and destiny. It can also very often, spiritually paralyze us. Many of us have experienced low self-esteem. We think so little of ourselves and believe the lies that we are worthy and deserving of the abuses we encounter, all because we have been conditioned to think so little of ourselves. Sometimes we are even blamed for what we are not guilty of. We are subsequently robbed of whom God created us to be. This was my personal experience until God healed and delivered me. I recalled embarrassing moments in my life when a compliment was extended to me, and I am sad to say that a compliment was like a death sentence to me.

For this very reason, many people subject themselves to continued abuse until the Lord opens our eyes and allows us to see who we are and who we are in Him.

This pattern of abuse is not God's plan for us, but if we look to Him, He will do everything to bring healing and restoration. My healing also included spiritual heart surgery, because of the severity of the woundedness of my heart. The Lord removed all the pain within, through spiritual surgery, cleaned me up, and subsequently poured His love into me and gave me a new heart. My old heart was too damaged for me to survive and most importantly, allow me to fulfill his call and destiny on my life and the Lord would have been robbed of His glory had I not been healed. With His divine intervention of healing, by removing all the damage within, and pouring His love into me, what the enemy tried to rob me of was instantly restored through the power of His love and this continued as I spent time in His Word and in His presence. Remember we learn daily, and He takes us from glory to glory each day.

While we experience diverse ways of learning to cope and heal, how wonderful and comforting to know that we have a Heavenly Father who sees all and knows just how much we can bear and how much we need. My heart was so broken and fragmented that I indeed needed His divine intervention and healing. You will learn more about this in later chapters.

There is more to our brokenness than we dare to imagine.

Woundedness and fragmentation of our soul causes much emotional damage and destruction within. It is only the Lord and the power of the Holy Spirit who sees all and can go deep within the recesses of our spirit to bring forth complete healing. God has given us all a promise, *"For I know the plans I have for you,' declares the Lord, 'plans to prosper you and not to harm you, plans to give you a hope and a future."* (Jeremiah 29:11 NIV) Let me emphasize His beautiful promise:

- He has a plan for us.
- He has a plan to prosper and not to harm us.
- He has a plan to give us a hope and a future.

I give thanks to the Lord that, His death on the Cross and resurrection from the grave brought us healing. *"But He was wounded for our transgressions, He was bruised for our iniquities; the chastisement of our peace was upon Him; and with His stripes we are healed."* (Isaiah 53:5 KJV)

We cannot experience God's blessings if we are broken and wounded. It is therefore beyond doubt that any other plans that cause us pain and brokenness are not from Him.

In His leading and guiding, my life was spared from physical death on many occasions. On one occasion, the police were informed by my ex-husband that his mission was "not to leave me alive." After the third time, the police were summoned to our matrimonial home, which he had abandoned and returned with a determination to take my life that night.

The Lord promises that He will never leave nor forsake us; He will be with us to the very end. He promises never to abandon us. Throughout that entire time, He was with me. He brought wonderful caring people into my life who became more than friends; they became family and even Godparents to my beloved son who was born during this troublesome marriage.

I give thanks every day for my loving and praying parents. Even though I was over four thousand miles away from home in a foreign country, they perceived I was in danger and prayed continuously for me. I will elaborate on this in a later chapter.

Journey with me as I share with you our Heavenly Father's mighty hand in my life during those dark and painful days. The blessings of his open and closed doors, clear instructions, His abiding presence, provisions, visitations, deliverances, and healings.

I pray this book brings healing and deliverance, hope, and restoration to you as it did for me knowing that we serve a mighty God who fights all our battles and gives us victory. He moves in ways we dare to think or imagine, beyond our normal understanding.

Pearl 1

The Awakening: Out of Bondage

"Awake, awake, put on thy strength, O Zion; put on thy beautiful garments, O Jerusalem, the holy city: for henceforth there shall no more come into thee the uncircumcised and the unclean." (Isaiah 52:1 KJV)

<u>What is bondage?</u>

According to Webster's Dictionary, bondage is captivity, servitude, or subjugation to a controlling person or force. Bondage is the enslavement of an individual to another person or an institution. This can be either spiritual, cultural, or physical bondage. Spiritual bondage refers to a concept in many religious and spiritual traditions that involves being bound or trapped by negative rules, regulations, entities, or beliefs that prevent one from achieving spiritual growth and liberation. Spiritual bondage can manifest in different ways, such as addiction, attachment to material possessions, harmful relationships, or negative thoughts and emotions. It can be overcome through practices such as meditation, prayer, counseling, and self-reflection, as well as by cultivating positive qualities such as compassion, forgiveness, and gratitude.

Throughout my life, I have experienced many spiritual bondages that kept me captive, stuck, bound, and restricted in various areas of my life. Have you ever felt like you were just existing and not truly living because you were unaware or afraid of your purpose? Being in bondage can strip you of who you really are called to be. In bondage, you lose your identity and purpose, and you can be completely derailed. What have you allowed to strip you of your identity and your purpose?

Culturally, I was raised under submission. Not submission only to my parents but to anyone in authority over my life. In my culture, I was even subjected to the authority of anyone older than me in my community, whether they were my family members or not. I did not have a choice but to be obedient and submissive to authority. I had to remain silent and only speak when spoken to. I could not allow myself to shine or be heard because I would be considered insubordinate or disrespectful. As you grow, mature, and start to expand outside of your community, you will quickly learn that you have been culturally bound. When I traveled to the United Kingdom and the United States, I quickly realized how much I missed out on in life. I was exposed to so many cultures, heritages, religions, beliefs, languages, and demographics that I never knew existed.

Subsequently, I was subjected to authoritative figures both physical and spiritual who sometimes had no understanding of the concept of submission and were in no position to lead. I was submissive to people back home because I could not go against my elders, family, and my culture. For example, in many countries, there are women whose husbands are chosen for them. They are stripped of their freedom to choose their own spouse. Out of both spiritual and physical bondage, I too got married due to my limited cultural beliefs and stayed in an abusive marriage because I was bound by the cultural norm that I was to never get a divorce because that is not of God.

Marriage was created to be a beautiful union between husband and wife, where there is a sincere love for each other accompanied by respect and trust. It should not be one of enslavement or bondage. Very often the abused individual does not see themselves as victims. They, unfortunately, accept the enslavement and subject themselves to the abuser out of fear or forced submission. They often feel very helpless and even blame themselves for the enslavement, believing that they did something wrong to deserve this treatment. In other words, they are brainwashed to believe they are the cause of this enslavement or emotional abuse.

In many cases, abusers are protected by the enslaved individual out of fear, guilt, or feeling undeserving of being treated affectionately. Victims also accept abuse due to the bondage of their past unhealed wounds, and most often a female is the victim of the abusive partner.

My personal 'Awakening from Bondage'

It was a lovely and bright Saturday evening two weeks after my marriage. As I sat quietly in my bedroom in Southwest London, the sun shone through brightly, and the gentle evening breeze blew through the opened window. Suddenly, however, I had a vision of myself with huge chain-links wrapped around me, from my neck to my feet. I saw myself in bondage.

It was without question, with much clarity, that I understood what the Lord was showing me. It was at that moment the Holy Spirit spoke clearly to my heart:

My daughter, you are in bondage. When you return to Jamaica, if you do not have your midwifery training, you will not be considered a fully qualified nurse. When your colleagues in Jamaica have completed their general nursing studies to qualify as registered nurses, they travel to England or Scotland to do their midwifery training. You are right here in the UK; make use of the opportunity and complete your studies in midwifery, as you will be expected and needed to deliver babies in your homeland." He continued, *"Do not do your studies here in London. I want you to return "home" where you will be far away, and you will be able to complete your studies without distractions and hindrances.*

"Home" for me in England was, and still is, Chelmsford, Essex. I have wonderful friends there and many treasured memories. I clearly observed that the Holy Spirit did not say to me, "if" but "when" you return to Jamaica. Nothing is hidden from the LORD. He knew the paths of restoration I had to take; hence, He was laying His plan of preparation and restoration out for me. This resonated deeply in my spirit, and I knew I had to obey His instructions. They were noticeably clear.

My immediate response was one of repentance because I knew exactly in my heart what I had done. I had entered a marriage that I should not have. I had not prayed earnestly about it. I presumptuously thought this was God's will for me.

Please forgive me Lord, I prayed. *I did not seek You for Your will in this decision. If You get me out of this, I will never do anything without seeking You.*

I began to have some second thoughts and regrets about entering this marriage, as suddenly there were some changes and unexplained negative behavior patterns in my ex-husband. What I once thought would be a lifetime of happiness was turning into a nightmare. I was beginning to feel very isolated and alone, as he spent many evenings and nights at the pub and weekends partying and drinking. I could not communicate with him because every conversation or interaction would become an argument with many accusations and condemnations with verbal threats. I began to lose my identity and developed feelings of great disappointment and poor self-worth, which began to overtake me. This was overwhelming because the mistreatment was without reason or explanation. They were episodes of sudden unexplained explosions with verbal and physical abuse.

I became very tearful during many sleepless nights and began to experience a loss of appetite and feelings of depression. Needless to say, in those times of loneliness and hopelessness, suicidal ideations began to set in. Feeling ashamed, I began to isolate myself from family and friends. I began to avoid social interactions and spent time alone out of fear. I had no one to turn to. I became confused and very disillusioned with the loss of what I perceived and anticipated to be a loving marital relationship. At the time, living in the United Kingdom (U.K.), it was taboo for one to experience relational problems, much less expose their marital problems. It was not talked about, so there were no outlets.

As much as possible, I made attempts to reason with my ex-husband to identify the source of our poor communication and the reason for his behavior so early in our marriage. Along with this, he experienced periods of unemployment, which left me the sole breadwinner. There were times when I felt unable to work due to the increasing stress and sleepless nights, and I also learned that he lied about his supposedly educational achievements, which was the reason for his inability to find sustainable employment.

Working as a nurse in cardiac intensive care required much accuracy and attention, and I struggled with this, as feelings of anxiety and loneliness began to take a toll on my health. To make matters worse, as I said before, I could not talk about it. It would have been shameful to do so.

Our home was an apartment within the house of our landlord. I learned that my ex-husband began to make many sexual advances to our landlord's young daughter. Both my landlord and his wife were very kind and supportive towards me, having witnessed the many episodes of my ex-husband's verbal abuse and late-night escapades. With regret, they asked us to vacate the apartment, with threats to take legal action against my ex if we did not leave the premises. I found this entire situation very shameful, embarrassing, and demoralizing with moments of feeling very helpless, hopeless, and paralyzed with fear. This is not what I hoped for. I felt completely abased with ruined self-esteem. This was out of my social standards and expectations, and I had no idea how to cope with it. This left me in a state of confusion, but I was still hoping and praying for a change in the situation. This is a mistake woman often make, as we believe we can change our spouses. We also stay in unhealthy relationships due to convenience and being bound by our culture and/or religion. I was young, far away from home, and I wanted so desperately to settle down and have a family of my own. Since I was abroad and felt isolated and alone.

I anxiously anticipated leaving home to continue my studies at midwifery school but would return on my days off where the abuse would continue.

We moved to a new apartment and in no time, I was able to make this a lovely and cozy home within my few days off from midwifery school. I thought our new environment and his promise to start over again would make things better.

It was after a late-night return home from the pub while drinking with friends that he became verbally aggressive. My hands were bound, and I was tied to a chair and beaten. He then threw me down in our matrimonial bed where I was sexually assaulted. His cold and callous response was, "This is what you need." I was crying hysterically while screaming for help. I tried with every might within me to resist, but this was a man who fought on the battlefields in the war of Northern Ireland and was strong enough to overpower me. I felt hopeless and helpless.

My return to school where I was a resident on campus was an immense help emotionally since I was away from the abusive surroundings and spent much time focusing on my studies. However, there were fearful moments returning home to London on my days off.

On many occasions upon my return to midwifery school, after no communication from my ex-husband and some overnight absence from home, I would receive a call from him to ensure that I had arrived at the nurse's quarters safely. Why? I wondered. It was much later, upon completing my studies and my permanent return to our home in London, that I learned this was to ensure I was safely out of the area so he could bring his girlfriend to our home.

On the first weekend of my return home, I was told of a new friend he wanted me to meet, whom I entertained with a lovely evening meal that Sunday afternoon. I was totally unaware that this was the woman he was having an affair with and who occupied our home and matrimonial bed in my absence. After learning this later that week, I was devastated and felt betrayed and violated. This was a deceptive plan to disguise their relationship as a cordial friendship, when in reality it was the continuation of their affair.

It was at this time my very close friends and my family became aware of what was going on, and from there, I had a lot of support, which was very helpful. My ex was very apologetic and kept expressing his desire for us to have a child to bring us closer and bring healing to our marriage. With much desire to save my marriage and establish the family and home I longed for, as well as "avoiding the shame," I agreed.

Even though the affair with this woman ended, as she was engaged to be married, his infidelity continued with other women. At this time, I discovered I was expecting our first child, which did not help the situation. After discovering that I was pregnant, he said he was not interested and advised me to abort our child, which I refused to do. He then decided to leave our marital home when I was three months pregnant. Honestly, this was a big relief for me. I was prepared to provide for this precious child in my womb and knew that God would make a way for us. I trusted that He would provide, knowing that all our finances in a joint savings account were completely depleted due to his many extramarital affairs. I was confident in my abilities in trying to save my marriage; however, I quickly learned that you cannot make someone love you or stay in a relationship beyond their will.

I had much support from friends, families, and church families in England. If you find someone in such a position as I found myself, as much as you can, offer help and support. It will be greatly appreciated, as I experienced.

I worked as a midwife until it was time for my maternity leave.

I was blessed with much support and understanding from my co-workers, who were extremely helpful and took the time to knit and crotchet many outfits, blankets, and all I needed for my baby.

It was during this time my ex discovered he was not comfortable living by himself in uncomfortable surroundings, unlike the comfort of our lovely and homey apartment, which I graciously decorated. He again apologized and expressed the desire to return home to "be a husband and father to our baby." For our son's sake and the frailty of our relationship, I refused. I became fearful that our child would experience abuse which I foresaw to be verbal, physical, mental, and emotional due to my ex's insecurity and insincerity. I became very protective of this child, and I could not expose him to that.

In retaliation for his unmet desires, he began his tirade of attacks against my life, and episodes of physical attack summoned me to call the police on two occasions. I was advised strongly by the police not to allow him to return to the apartment due to his aggressive and threatening behavior.

Four months after our son was born, he again expressed the desire to return to us. With this again not granted, he became aggressive and made many attempts to break into my apartment. I was alone with our infant son. Upon calls and advice from my neighbor, whom my ex-husband informed of his plan to kill me if he was not allowed to return, I called the local police and was immediately connected to Scotland

Yard, which is the headquarters for the London Metropolitan Police. After a few calls to the local police, subsequent calls would immediately be transferred to them.

They were very kind, helpful, and supportive and immediately dispatched the local police as they promised. It was then my ex reported to them that his intention was not to leave me alive that night; he came to kill me. An attempt to incarcerate him that night was made by the police due to the threat on my life. I pleaded with them as I dreaded the thought of my son's father being incarcerated. He was warned of their plans to make many surveillances, and if he was found in the area, he would be arrested.

It was that night that I cried out desperately to the Lord for help, as I knew I had to move away out of fear for my life and the safety of both me and my son. I became afraid, especially for the welfare of our son. I dreaded the thought of my innocent and precious infant son being placed in and raised in foster homes. In my desperation, I cried out to Him and said, *Lord, if you do not help me, who else will? I am far away from home where my parents would help me. I have no one to turn to, but you!!*

After contacting my siblings about this occurrence, I expressed my need for help to return home to Jamaica where I knew I would be safe. They graciously offered to help me, and the following day, I began to make active and drastic plans and arrangements. I can never thank my parents enough for their love and prayer-covering during this time.

I was afraid to inform them of the severity of my broken marriage, even though they observed that things were not as they were supposed to be, and I did not release information to them in its entirety for fear of causing them to worry due to being so far away.

It was during this time that both my parents, who are devout intercessors who earnestly prayed without ceasing for their children, began to discern that "something was wrong with one of us," as they later reported. I learned that my father was not able to sleep for at least three nights in succession as he discerned "someone was in danger."

During this time, my mother had a dream that both her and my father received a call from the airport authorities to retrieve my body, which was sent home in a casket. She said they picked up my body but refused to bury me, while many went to our home in mourning. I thanked her for their prayers and refusal to bury me because if they did, I would indeed have been killed.

Within four weeks, my darling infant son Chris and I safely arrived at my parent's home in Jamaica. I worked in the local hospital for two years until I returned to the U.K., as instructed by the Holy Spirit, to pursue a course in psychiatry with plans to move to the United States of America (USA). Honestly, this was against my plans, but the Lord, to whom I entrusted my life and the life of my son, was working things out, and it was very important for me to obey. I strongly sensed His leading and direction for restoration and plans for providing for my son and myself.

My parents fully supported me with this venture and offered to take care of my son Chris until I was able to settle down. He remained with them for another four years. This was an exceedingly difficult time for me, as I missed him terribly, but I comforted myself by affirming that I was doing this in order to prepare for our future.

Case Study on Bondage

I recall a situation many years ago while working overseas where I was informed of a new patient admission. I found the doctor's drastic procedures for the patient's well-being very strange, but at the same time, I understood why. My patient was part of a tightly bonded race and community with extraordinarily strong religious and cultural beliefs, and so was the doctor.

She said she was verbally and physically abused by her husband, mother-in-law, and father-in-law, with whom she lived. Her mother-in-law and husband often beat her and treated her like a "Cinderella," as she stated. She had to do all the housework as well as take care of her two young children and her mother-in-law without any help, and when not completed, she was severely beaten.

She was brought into the emergency room with a broken arm, cuts, and bruises, and she was two months pregnant. She was also very tearful and depressed.

Despite their cultural and religious beliefs about abortion, in this desperate situation, the termination of pregnancy was performed by this very caring and devoted doctor. Again, this was totally against both the doctor's and the patient's spiritual and moral beliefs, but the doctor felt this was best for both her patient and the young fetus.

As is common with abused persons, my patient was very withdrawn and isolated from her parents and siblings. She did not nor could she call them from home; (at that time, there were no cell phones, only landlines). Her father stated that he found it very strange that she always called from the public pay phone, only to discover that she was afraid to call from her home. As a caring father, he stepped in with full support and care for his daughter and grandchildren.

<u>Signs of Bondage</u>

- Victim experiences fear of physical or psychological threats, like losing their life, children, or financial support
- Manipulative behaviors of the abuser, such as repeated and temporary episodes of small acts of kindness; false hope for improvement in the relationship
- Physical and emotional blackmail
- Religious or cultural beliefs or expectations to disguise abusive behavior

- Unexplained or irrelevant excuses for absences from occasions such as family gatherings
- Isolation from family and friends and no social life
- Signs of depression
- Loss of weight and appetite
- Insomnia due to stress
- Sexual abuse
- Obvious signs of physical abuse, such as bruises or sometimes broken limbs
- Forced to do things against your will or conscience
- Always feeling afraid and timid
- Abuser is often very loud, controlling, and manipulative
- Lies and deceptive behavior
- Controlling behaviors like monitoring partners' daily activities through their devices

- Searching partners' mobile devices to monitor their communication
- Abuser's complete control of finances and family estate
- Marital affairs or cheating
- Blaming spouse for affairs due to guilt
- Drug and alcohol abuse
- History of childhood abuse or poor family structure
- Having firsthand experienced abuse within their family

You can only be absolutely free when you can realize and acknowledge that you're enslaved to bondage. It is only when we receive an understanding of a situation that we will be set free from its bondage. Bondage is designed to rob, derail, paralyze, and imprison. It robs us of our destinies and purpose in life.

Being set free delivers and liberates us. It provides great wisdom, knowledge, and understanding. Bondage is a spiritual blindfold that is meant to stagnate and render us powerless and ineffective. It overshadows us with darkness, doubt, insecurity, and fear. It causes severe darkness and deadness of the soul, thus making wisdom and discernment more difficult to experience.

It is bound and decorated with lies and deception. When we are free, we are truly and forever free and can no longer be deceived. We see the truth for what it really is. Wisdom and discernment are imparted and the veil which separates us is destroyed. We can then freely enter the places and spaces God has designed us to be.

Bondage causes us to operate in deception. It stifles, suffocates, and imprisons us. It locks us out of the door of God's promises and blessings and closes the door to an effective prayer life and even healthy relationships. It causes us to assume, instead of seeing and knowing the truth in which lies our freedom.

If you identify yourself to be in bondage, remember that God wants to set you free and not to be bound or oppressed in any way, shape, or form. He is always open to our prayers and cries for help.

Escaping Bondage

How does one escape an emotionally abusive situation? Many will tell you to get out, but it is not always that simple due to feelings of fear, hopelessness, helplessness, and loss of confidence and control. Sometimes, the situation becomes too familiar.

One may also feel very confused, torn, and uncertain of the future, with fears of inability to cope on their own. Sometimes victims hold on for fear of having a failed relationship, especially in the case of marriage, or they hold on for the children's sake.

Breaking free from bondage can be an incredibly difficult, painful, and threatening journey. The wounds caused by the bondage may run deep, and it can be overwhelming to confront them, but know that you are not alone in your struggle. There is hope for healing and growth, and you deserve to experience a life free from the chains that have held you back.

As you embark on this journey, it's normal to experience a mix of emotions — fear, anger, sadness, regrets, and perhaps even relief at finally acknowledging the bondage. You may feel vulnerable and exposed as you begin to peel back the layers of pain and trauma. However, please know that facing these feelings is a brave and powerful step toward your healing.

It's okay to ask for help and support during this time. You do not have to go through this alone. Seek out trusted friends, family members, or professionals who can help to guide you on your journey. They can offer a listening ear, a safe space to process your emotions, and resources to help you develop healthy coping mechanisms.

Remember that healing takes time, and it's important to be gentle with yourself. Grant yourself grace because this journey is not an overnight process. God promises never to leave or forsake us, and He'll be with us until the very end. According to Deuteronomy 31:6-7 (KJV), "Be strong and of a good courage, fear not, nor be afraid of them: for the LORD thy God, he it is that doth go with thee; he will not fail thee, nor forsake thee."

Remind yourself of the following affirmations daily:

- You are worthy of love.
- You are beautiful and powerful beyond what you think.
- You are not the blame for being battered or mistreated.
- You are not the cause of your partner's abusive behavior.
- You are deserving of love and to be with the best purpose partner God has for you.
- You deserve to be treated with respect.
- You deserve a safe, peaceful, and happy life.
- Your children also deserve a safe and happy life.
- You should never settle for less in life out of fear, insecurities, and thoughts of unworthiness.
- You are not alone. There are people waiting to help who have been through what you're going through.

"If the Son therefore shall make you free, ye shall be free indeed"
(*John 8:36 KJV*)

My Prayer For Us

Heavenly Father, I thank you for your Word. I thank You for Your only begotten Son, our Lord Jesus Christ, who died on the cross to set me free. I receive Your plan of Redemption, deliverance, and healing from every form of bondage.

I ask You Heavenly Father to deliver us from every form of bondage. Please deliver us from fear, oppression, and any form of hindrances in our lives. Thank You for your promises to set us free. You said, "If the Son therefore shall make you free, ye shall be free indeed" (John 8:36 KJV). I thank you for my freedom.

Thank you, Heavenly Father, for not leaving nor forsaking us. Today, we receive that promise and stand on your words. Thank You for setting us free in the mighty and precious name of Jesus, we pray, with thanksgiving.

Thank you, Heavenly Father.
Amen

Pearl 2
God's Healing and Promises

"Trust in the Lord with all thine heart; and lean not unto thine own understanding. In all thy ways acknowledge Him and He will direct thy paths" (Proverbs 3:5-6 KJV).

Have you been in a place where you were afraid and felt there was no help or hope for you? I know that place, and through those challenging times, I totally surrendered to the Lord to help, lead, and guide me. I had no choice; He was my only hope for strength, peace, and deliverance.

I know many of you, my readers, have been in that place — some to a lesser degree and some even worse. Some with not only one child but more. I want to share with you that the Lord will never abandon you. He has promised in His Word, "The Lord is close to the brokenhearted, and saves those who are crushed in spirit" (Psalm 34:18 NIV). When we are at our lowest, that is when He is closer to us. He loves and cares for us too much to abandon us.

It was during this time of brokenness that I experienced so much help, even from strangers who became familiar with my situation through family and friends.

During the difficult time of being away from my precious son Chris, the Lord gave me the comforting word from Proverbs 3:5-6. This brought so much comfort and strength to my troubled soul. He comforted me with the promise that He would take care of my son, be a Father to him, and prosper him. He has been faithful to His promise. I totally surrendered to the Lord's instructions as He opened and closed doors. It was during this time I experienced numerous miracles and divine visitations from Him.

With instructions to return to England to pursue a course in clinical psychiatry, He opened the impossible door for acceptance at Leeds University Hospital in Leeds, U.K. After my three months of studies, He gave me clear instructions to work within a pediatric facility. This was neither my favorite nor strong area, so the experience was very helpful.

It was after a visitation from the Lord, who spoke to me about becoming a head nurse, that I was approached the following day by the director of the OBGYN department who made me the offer. During this time, I was in the process of making plans through an agency that was recruiting nurses to the USA. I was afraid to take this position, knowing that I was making plans to travel to the USA. The Lord spoke to my heart that my application and work visa would take approximately eighteen months to be processed. There would be a waiting period; hence, I was to take this position, and it would add tremendously to my resume. Indeed, it took eighteen months for my application and visa to be processed for my new job with the Medical College of Virginia Hospitals in Virginia. This is a true testimony of what it is like to stand on God's promises and trust His word. Also, for you my readers, as He has promised, He will never leave nor forsake you. I experienced His divine guidance with His visitations, accompanied by opened and closed doors as well as favor throughout this entire situation.

To embrace God's promises and trust my journey of healing, I had to realize and acknowledge my hurt and how far away I was from enjoying peace in my life. I became aware and knowledgeable of the person I was dealing with. "For we wrestle not against flesh and blood, but against principalities, against powers, against the rulers of the darkness of this world, against spiritual wickedness in high places" (*Ephesians 6:12 KJV*).

Most times the people around us and those in our lives have issues and problems they are not aware of. They are unaware of how controlled they are by the principalities that govern and dictate their lives, especially if they are not surrendered to the Lord. They are bound with an unregenerated or born-again spirit. They live and operate according to the dictates of their flesh and are incapable of giving and most often cannot receive love.

Many are laden with cares and burdens and operate from the burdens they carry. There is only bondage and no freedom in their spirit.

Such connections can cause us to lose sight of who we are and cause us to be enslaved to unhealthy relationships because we too become enablers and thus become trapped. Here we lose our identity and may sometimes become powerless to be free from such entrapment. Sometimes the relationship becomes too familiar, and we feel bound to it, as will be discussed later with soul ties.

We must be aware of when we are starting to lose our identity. This is where we find ourselves bound and trapped in a relationship until our spiritual eyes are opened. This weakens us and strips us of our identity and who we truly are.

I was being stripped of who I was and who I wanted to be. I started recognizing my ex's anger and his need to be vindictive and retaliatory. He always said to me, "My mother was not happy, so what makes you think you would be happy?" This statement was the final limit for me. It proved to me that he had no intention of changing and was bent on taking his anger out on me. We owe it to ourselves to be happy. Recognizing that I had the potential to experience peace and freedom from within was my final decision to break loose from this bondage.

Journey to Freedom

My journey of healing and self-preservation started when I chose to protect my life and the well-being of my infant son. I had to take into consideration that I was not alone, and there were loved ones who genuinely cared for us and were concerned for my safety. The meaningful change for me came when the Lord opened my eyes to discern and understand what and whom I was dealing with. Another crucial factor was the loss of my peace and identity.

I do not have words enough to thank the Lord for His guidance and deliverance throughout this entire ordeal. My eyes were opened to the fact that I had been trusting in my own might and desires instead of the Lord's. A vital scripture and powerful road map for me was the word and counsel He gave in a moment of hopelessness and desperation from Proverbs 3:5-6 (KJV), "Trust in the Lord with all your heart and lean not to your own understanding. In all your ways acknowledge Him and He will direct your paths." This scripture literally jumped off the pages of the Bible and spoke directly and loudly to me.

It was also a bondage breaker for me and increased my surrender and trust in the Lord. I felt like a child holding unto Daddy's hand and being led to safety. I sensed and experienced such love, protection, and provision.

To be honest, having been so crushed, wounded, and disappointed, I had no intentions of meeting anyone, nor did I have the desire to be married again.

My plan was to move to the United States as I was instructed by the Lord and prepare to raise my son by myself. This changed three months after my arrival in the USA. Through God's divine plan and orchestration, I met my now husband, Tom. We met in the laundry room of the large apartment complex where we both lived. It may seem strange, but it was indeed "love at first sight."

As my interest grew, I applied for a divorce, which was speedily granted. After ten months of having met and dated, Tom asked me to be his wife, and we got married six months later. During our time of dating, Tom made travel arrangements for my son Chris to visit with him so they could cultivate a relationship. Chris had never met his father, so he was more than happy to meet Tom, who adopted him soon after we were married. Chris joined us for our wedding and graciously, at six years of age, served as our ring bearer.

My son, Chris, as my ring bearer.

Since then, Chris has become a loving and caring older brother to his younger two brothers and only sister, all of whom Tom and I had together. They are all now grown and married and have given us five lovely grandchildren and a bonus grandson — the joys of our hearts. Our blessed union has brought us forty years of wonderful marital bliss with a lovely growing family (up to the time of writing this book in 2023).

Remind yourself that you are a powerful conqueror, and the secret weapon is hidden deep within you. You have the tools to stand up against any bondage through Christ Jesus. You are not weak for struggling, and it is okay to take breaks and step back when needed. Keep in mind that the road ahead may be difficult, but the reward of a life free from bondage is immeasurable. You are worthy of healing and growth. You have the strength and resilience to overcome this bondage, and I believe in you.

Take note of God's opened and closed doors and the people He brings into your life. These are unbelievably valuable in the process of healing and restoration.

Chris served in the military and graduated with honors in July 2022

My Calling to be a Nurse

From a young age, I aspired to walk in my mother's footsteps. She was a devoted homemaker, dedicating her life to nurturing her children with love and care. She embodied the qualities of a compassionate and protective Christian mother. I remember a moment in my biology class when I questioned the relevance of my studies, considering my deep-rooted desire to follow in my mother's path as a homemaker. Unbeknownst to me, the Lord had a different plan, leading me into the medical field, where I found immense fulfillment, serving Him to the best of my abilities.

My journey took an unexpected turn with my marriage to my ex-husband, compelling me to make a hasty decision driven by my desire to mirror my mother's life. I yearned to realize the childhood dream of becoming a wife and mother, inspired by the example she had set.

As a young girl, the Lord must have planted that seed of being a Nurse in my spirit, as my play time included running a "medical clinic," which was held at the back of our home under an orange tree. I used the thorns from a particular orange tree for my injection needles and scraps from my mother's sewing were used for my cleaning swabs. My friends in the neighborhood were my patients, and they would come to my "clinic" for their injections.

I developed such an interest in visiting the sick in the hospital in my hometown and had so much compassion for them during their suffering. I spent many hours after high school visiting, helping, and praying for them.

After high school, I was granted the privilege to attend nursing school through an overseas recruiting program and was admitted to Chelmsford and Essex School of Nursing, now East Anglia University, after a brief course of studies in London.

As a student in high school, I received a bursary from Christ Church United Reformed Church, London Road, Chelmsford, Essex UK. I had a pen pal there, an older lady, who eventually became an incredibly good friend and mentor. I chose to attend nursing school there in order to fellowship with the family at Christ Church United Reform Church (URC).

During my time of studies, I became a regular and active member of the church, and it was also a blessing and an honor to have sung in the choir. I was welcomed as a daughter among many older members, including my pastor and his beloved wife, now deceased. Their homes were homes away from home for me, and some even visited with me after I immigrated to the USA. They considered it a blessing to have had me worshiping with them after so many years of helping me with my high school education at Clarendon College in

Jamaica. It was a dream come true for me. After so many years of communication and thank you letters for their financial support, I was finally able to meet these wonderful and kind people; hence, Chelmsford became a haven for me.

As a young girl, I was raised in an extremely strict Christian home. It was therefore important for me to have a spouse who loved and feared the Lord. When a foundation is laid in one's life, we often maintain that lifestyle. Scripture tells us, "Train up a child in the way he should go; and when he is old, he will not depart from it" (*Proverbs 22:6 KJV*). I found that to be true, as things I was not allowed to do, even though I was far away from home, did not appeal to me, and the principles I was raised with remained part of my lifestyle. Needless to say, we know that is not always the case. There are situations in our lives that sometimes cause us to make bad decisions, and I know that was my situation, but I still give thanks for that foundation which I held dear and which was a compass for me.

With many of my colleagues from overseas at that time, I observed many disastrous consequences from partying. Not only did this habit affect their studies, but it caused many setbacks and unplanned responsibilities such as raising families out of wedlock, the end of their studies, and financial difficulties. This also affected their parents back home, as they faced many disappointments and shame according to my colleagues.

Partying became a frequent and dangerous habit among many, which was sometimes caused by loneliness and homesickness, but it was encouraged by others to "just have fun and party." This is said with no condemnation to my friends and colleagues. Living in a foreign land without our close families can be incredibly challenging, and unless we are firmly grounded, we are prone to mistakes. Living so far away from home was difficult for many of us. Homesickness was quite common, and sometimes friendships were sought in the wrong places and with the wrong individuals.

It was remarkably interesting and very educational to have met so many friends from all over the world while in nursing school and to also observe and learn from the many areas of heartache we all experienced. Among us, we fought many battles with many decisions to make, but we always supported each other toward the completion of our schoolwork and graduation.

God's Promises According to His Word

Have you ever stopped to think or ask yourself what are God's promises for you? God has a plan and a purpose for each one of us. We are not here to sit idly on earth not walking in our purpose. He has a plan for each of us for our benefit and for His glory; *"For all the promises of God in Him are yea, and in Him Amen, unto the glory of God by us."* (2 Corinthians 1:20 KJV)

This means that His promises are established, sure, and firm. According to Numbers 23:19 (KJV*), "God is not a man that He should lie, nor a son of man that He should repent. Hath He said and shall he not do it? Hath He not spoken, and shall He not make it good?"*

He knows us completely and does not make excuses for the promises He has made to us, so what is right and fitting for us shall come to pass. It is for us to obey His instructions, and we will see them manifested to His glory.

We can think of many promises spoken to the patriots in the Bible but let us look at one example in Genesis 12:1-3, where God blessed Abram as He established a nation for His glory:

"Now the LORD said unto Abram, get thee out of thy country, and from thy kindred, and from thy father's house, unto a land that I will shew thee; and I will make of thee a great nation, and I will bless thee, and make thy name great; and thou shalt be a blessing: and I will bless them

that bless thee, and curse him that curseth thee: and in thee shall all families of the earth be blessed." (Genesis 12:1-3 KJV)

These were the words that were spoken to Abram by God before his name was changed to Abraham. That promise still stands today with the Jewish nation. They are blessed, and God has used them for His glory, and so it is with us Gentiles and all who call upon His name.

The Lord's name is great and powerful, yet He says He has established His Word (His promises) above His name; "I will worship toward thy Holy temple and praise Thy name for thy lovingkindness and for thy truth: for thou hast magnified thy word above all thy name" (Psalm 138:2 KJV). This tells us how powerful God's word is and that He watches over them to bring them to pass.

The promises spoken to us in His Word and to our hearts are there to lead and guide us. He will not allow us to wander aimlessly, hence He has given us sure, established, and secure instructions that make up the blueprint of our lives. God's Word is a lamp unto our feet and a light to our path. This leads and guides us to the right places. (See Psalm 119:105).

He promised to deliver the Children of Israel out of bondage in Egypt, and as they wandered through the wilderness into the promised land, He was with them in the form of a pillar of cloud by day and a pillar of fire by night.

We can rest in God's promises, for they are sure. There is no need to question them. Sometimes they may seem completely out of our ability to receive or comprehend. We may not see ourselves as capable or worthy of His awesome promises spoken to us. It is here we must trust Him who is the author and finisher of our faith, according to Hebrews 12:2. He is the one who has written the details of our lives and will gently lead us through them.

We must also exercise patience and wait patiently for Him to see His promises come to pass. We should avoid birthing an "Ishmael."

In Genesis 17, God was establishing a covenant with Abram to multiply him exceedingly. God promised to do even what seemed impossible with his wife Sarai (Sarah) who was beyond childbearing years. He promised Sarai that she would be "a mother of nations" (Genesis 17:16 KJV) and conceive her first child, who was to be called Isaac, at 90 years old. However, Sarai did not believe she could bear a child at her age. They waited but became impatient and could no longer wait on Him for the promised child. So, they chose to take matters into their own hands and to do it their way by allowing Sarai's maidservant, Hagar, to birth their child as a surrogate, which was completely out of God's purpose and plans. Hagar gave birth to a baby boy named Ishmael, but he was not the promised child. This was a notable example of what a lack of trust and faith in God's promises looks like. Sarah embodied fear and doubt, which most of us can relate to, including myself.

We see this happen quite often when we choose not to wait on

God for His promises to be established in our lives. We compromise, thus making the wrong choices and facing multiple problems, which may last for generations as was seen in the situation with Ishmael.

We must not kindle our own fire believing this is God's fire for us because we will suffer the consequences such as derailments, abandonments, pain, and heartache. This is the outcome of many situations in life, especially in the case of broken marriages. Not only do we end up with broken and fragmented hearts, but our children and children's children for generations can be affected as a generational curse is established instead of a covenant blessing.

Although Sarai and Abram were disobedient, God still showed them favor and blessed them with the promised child, Isaac. This is a fitting example of God keeping His promises, despite our disobedience and lack of trust in Him. We see the continued feud that has gone on for generations through the families of the covenant son of a promise, Isaac, and the surrogate son, Ishmael.

God has a perfect plan and choice of a life-long, purposeful spouse for each of us. It is important to be prayerful and observant so as not to bring an "Ishmael" into our lives. This causes much pain and destiny failures.

Self-Reflection:

How many times have we given birth to an Ismael?

_____

_____

Has God promised you an Isaac blessing, but through lack of faith and unbelief, you birth an Ismael instead or simply miscarried what He purposed in you?

_____

_____

Again, I ask the question, what promises are you waiting for?

_____

_____

Are you willing to wait, despite your circumstances, so you can birth God's promises to your life?

_____

_____

Are you waiting for a spouse and believing God for the person he has prepared for you, instead of making your own decision?

_____

_____

What are the hindrances to walking in God's promises?

- Doubt
- Fear
- Unbelief
- Feeling unworthy
- Impatience
- Sin

God's promises and blessings are to bring us peace and joy, not pain and sorrow. Oftentimes, my mentees in God's Precious Pearl Ministry ask me, "How do I know which way to go or when it's God's way?" My answer to them is to always be led by God's peace. Be patient and obedient to the promises He has spoken to you. Even if you are not as spiritually mature and don't quite know how to recognize God's voice and direction, always do what gives you peace, and do not be led by the spirit of confusion. Try to avoid being lukewarm with a wavering spirit. God has not given us a spirit of fear but of power, love, and a sound mind, according to 2 Timothy 1:7. Be led by a sound mind, and walk with power, love, and authority so you can birth God's promises in your life. Continue to pray and give Him thanks daily. Allowing yourself to be led with gratitude positions you for His blessings over your family, finances, career, health, relationships, and everything pertaining to you. God promises to make perfect the things that concern us, as affirmed in Psalm 139:8. We must choose to walk in His perfect will, and we will never lack nor compromise.

Pearl 3
The Call

Do you know God's plan and purpose for your life?

Do you know what the calling on your life is?

Well, one morning while in my deep sleep, the Lord woke me up and began to speak to my heart about His calling on my life — His Purpose. Please join me in my journey as I share with you the exact words the Lord spoke to my heart in regard to my calling:

Dear Daughter,

I have called you to minister to those who are hurting, wounded, and do not know how to seek healing. If you have not experienced this, you cannot reach out to those in similar circumstances. You are like a Pearl that has been formed within the shell of an oyster due to irritation from a parasite or grain of sand. There are women hurting everywhere and in different areas of their lives. There are also those who have been beaten up by the world and the Church.

I, Myself, have experienced hurt, and I have allowed you to experience it too, and I am anointing you in these areas so you can lead from experience. Women will come to you from afar because they have heard of you, and I will send them to you. There you will impart my healing to them.

Indeed, I have called your home a place of refuge because I will send them to you where they will receive healing. Remember the key is to remain in love despite their wounds. Do not allow painful situations to cause you to walk out of love.

See My hand in every painful situation. Share your hurt with Me, your disappointments, and your pain. No one else knows about them like I do because no one else can see them as I do. No one knows your heart like I do. Many will think they do, but they really do not. I am the only One who truly discerns your heart.

Your heart, my daughter, belongs to Me. I formed it, so I will nurture and protect it. I will only allow you to share it with whom I instruct you to share it with. There are many ravenous wolves who would only desire to tear you apart, attempting to make you useless in My Kingdom. Hence, I instruct you to guard your heart and not to cast your pearls before swine. They will only trample on you and destroy all that I have placed within you.

There is a remnant that I have set apart for My purpose and My glory… a purpose in this hour. I, therefore, call you to walk always in love and in My wisdom. Remain always in My Word, which will lead, guide, and instruct you. Live a quiet and peaceful life. Rid yourself of worry, frustration, and distractions. Rid yourself of anything that may disturb your peace.

Always be still so you will hear My gentle voice. I am your source of strength and refuge. Look only to Me, and you will always find guidance in Me.

I am calling my people to be vigilant. Much wisdom and discernment are needed in this hour and during these difficult times. Much trust and waiting on Me is needed. The darkness is increasing. Rid yourselves of any elements of darkness. Do not entertain nor partake of its resources. My arms are outstretched to receive and protect you from the encroaching darkness. Walk away, trust, and look to Me. I am your source.

Pray for peace and deliverance from the stormy clouds that are encroaching. Whatever I tell you to do, do it and you will experience my peace.

I love you,

Abba Father

Scripture

"For those God foreknew, He also predestined to be conformed to the image of His Son, that He might be the firstborn among many brothers and sisters. And those He predestined, these He also called, whom He called, these He also justified; and whom He justified, these He also glorified" (Romans 8:29-30 NIV*).*

Personal Reflection from the Call

As I asked earlier, do you know God's calling and plan for your life? Those words that the Holy Spirit spoke to me were clear and resonated deeply in my spirit. When God shared with me my calling and His plans for my life, I honestly felt humbled, yet unworthy and unprepared. I am sure many of you can relate to this. When God reveals our purpose to us, sometimes we avoid, dismiss, or doubt His instructions.

His instructions came with such an assurance that was accompanied by the peace of the Holy Spirit despite my fear. I also sensed deep within my spirit a feeling of passion with a purpose, a goal with the awareness of establishing discipline to spend more time with the Lord in order to receive clear directions from Him. I was assured of a more meaningful purpose in life and began to clearly understand the reasons for the pains and struggles I faced, especially in the areas of relational brokenness. I had to be crushed for the oil of His anointing to come forth: "But He knoweth the way that I take; when He hath tried me, I shall come forth as gold" (Job 23:10 KJV).

There was no need to be angry or remorseful, nor reflect negatively on my past hurts. I began to recognize and accept it as my training ground, which some may call "The School of Hard Knocks." God knows we live in a sinful world, and we will face many trials, pains, and disappointments. I felt the love and comfort of the LORD, and it gave me a feeling of peace and rest in Him.

As we submit to Him, trusting Him for healing and deliverance, He will allow us to use them for His glory. I was reminded of His Word from 2 Corinthians:

Blessed be God, even the Father of our Lord Jesus Christ, the Father of mercies, and the God of all comfort; who comforteth us in all our tribulation, that we may be able to comfort them which are in any trouble, by the comfort wherewith we ourselves are comforted of God. For as the sufferings of Christ abound in us, so our consolation also aboundeth by Christ. And whether we be afflicted, it is for your consolation and salvation, which is effectual in the enduring of the same sufferings which we also suffer: or whether we be comforted, it is for your consolation and salvation. (2 Corinthians 1:3-6 KJV)

I was assured that all the pain, disappointments, and brokenness I experienced was not in vain but for the glory of God. My sufferings were not allowed to destroy me. I looked to the only One I knew who could help me. I cried out to Him and entrusted my life to Him; "And they overcame him by the blood of the Lamb, and by the word of their testimony, and they loved not their lives unto the death" (*Revelation 12:11 KJV*).

The Holy Spirit also confirmed His call on my life with His Word from Isaiah 61 — the call to heal the brokenhearted and set the captives free. It became such a part of me that I couldn't walk away from it or question it. I choose to submit myself to Him for His instruction and guidance. It was not a man who spoke to my heart; it was God, and this meant so much more to me.

Even with the unworthiness that I sensed, there was joy and excitement within, with an assured feeling of love and acceptance from the Lord. If this has spoken to you and tugged on your heart, God wants me to encourage you to seek Him for your calling. God has a plan for all of us. He will use your suffering and your trials as your testimony for His glory and your pain for His purpose. God downloaded a message in my spirit for you saying the following:

Blessed are you my child because I have called you and appointed you. Do not fear what men may say about you. Only look to me, the One who knows you. I am the One who searches the hearts of all men. I see your heart, and I know your thoughts. Trust me, I know everything. You have cried, you have wept deeply within your soul. I have seen the pain. I have seen your deep sorrow which leads to repentance. This one thing I ask of you is to hold my hand, stay close to Me, and fearlessly trust Me, and I will see you through. I hold the keys to the gates, and I will show you. I will open the gates wide for you to enter. No man has the power to hold the keys; they do not know the combination. I know the combination, and as you look to Me, trust Me, and depend on Me, I will show you how to gain full access. Do not lose heart; brighter days in Me are ahead. Not brighter days for the world and those who do not know Me and My hope, but for those who know and seek Me. Rise up from the grave of fear and despair. Look to Me whose face is radiant and full of hope. All fears disappear in My presence, all hope is in Me, so trust Me little one, I love you. Know this and hope in this, that I am always with you and as long as you trust, hope, and call on Me, I will be with you. I see the longing in your heart, I see the pain, and I see the fear. Rest in Me, trust Me, I am your all in all.I am Your Hope, your Strength, and your Refuge. I am your Hiding place, hide in Me. Give Me all your cares and fears and replace them with hope in Me.I am with you and all those dear to you. I hear your cries for those dear to you. They too are my concern, so do not lose hope in them. I stand by them as well. Now rest in Me and trust in Me and move on. Follow My path and move on with Me. I am your guide and the ultimate navigation, your GPS. Blessed little one, I am with you.

Love,

Abba Father

Scripture Reference

Psalm 34:4,5, 8
Psalm 40:2
Psalm 134:7
Jeremiah 29:11
Romans 29:30
2 Corinthians 7:10
Revelation 1:18

Prayer

Heavenly Father, I thank you that before I was formed in my mother's womb, you had a plan for my life. Thank you for keeping me under Your watchful care, for healing, and for delivering me from all my pain and sorrows. You saw me fit for your purpose in spite of my flaws and weaknesses. Although I have many shortcomings, you still found me worthy of representing your Kingdom. You still called me and for that, I am so grateful, Father. Lord, please help me to respond boldly to the call as I lead others to you. Please help me to always rest in You, trust You, and obey You. You have called me to those who are broken and have lost all hope. Continue to guide me as you equip me for your "Precious Pearls." Thank You for Jesus. You hold the keys to my life and to the Holy Spirit who is my teacher, counselor, and guide. I will continue to stand on your promises and abide in your shadow as you lead me.

In the precious Name of Jesus, I pray.

Amen.

Pearl 4
Responding To Your Calling

It is only by meditating on God's Word that we behold His Glory. When the Virgin Mary meditated and pondered on the message from the Angel, our Lord Jesus was conceived in her womb. After the seed was conceived through believing, she isolated herself from everyone and went to the hillside of Judea with her cousin Elizabeth, who was also pregnant, and Elizabeth's husband, the Priest Zachariah. (See Luke Chapter 1.)

We must not only read the Word, but we must also meditate and ponder on it and allow it to be conceived or become rhema within us. The Word of God is a powerful spiritual seed, and from this we will see a bountiful spiritual harvest.

Like Mary, we too must separate ourselves and be with like-minded people with a similar calling. It is also important to note that it is after the first trimester, which is the first three months of pregnancy, that the fetus is anchored within the womb. The placenta, which is the main anchor that supports and transfers nutrients to the developing infant, takes the first three months to be anchored to the uterine wall. All nutrients are received from the mother through her rich blood supply. We too must be anchored to God to receive our vast supply. There are many factors that may prevent this from happening.

Mary was a young girl who was engaged to be married, and here she was pregnant. By the law at that time, she could have been subjected to death by stoning, not to mention the many other accusations and ills that could cause a disruption in this initial and vital process of fetal development.

We too must hide away with the Holy Spirit and allow spiritual conception to take place. If not, the enemy will use many ways to cause a spiritual abortion. Many of us have been delayed in our calling, and I must admit to having been delayed due to many distractions. Be mindful of the fact that some of what appears to have been "Divine appointments," even in service within the Body of Christ, were for the wrong reasons. What may have seemed to be a "God idea" was very often man's idea. We end up birthing an Ishmael which causes spiritual abuse, heartache, and derailment. Do not lose heart, for the Lord saw your heart that longed to serve Him. I bear witness that He will heal and restore you. The first step is to forgive.

The placenta acts like the Holy Spirit in our spiritual development; it nourishes, teaches, and protects us. We must be hidden in God's Word and in prayer, which I see as the amniotic fluid that buffers and protects the baby.

Isaiah, who was called by God to be a prophet to the nations, received revelation after he beheld the glory and majesty of the Lord. It was in the glory that his eyes were opened to his sins and the sins of the people among whom he dwelt. The Word of God will do the same to us.

We will behold His Glory and be made aware of our sins and the sins around us. This is important before we can move into the call on our lives.

In Isaiah 6:5, the prophet said, "Woe is me, for I am undone! Because I am a man of unclean lips, and I dwell in the midst of a people of unclean lips; for my eyes have seen the King, The LORD of hosts" (Isaiah 6:5 KJV).

It is only in the presence of the Lord as we behold His awesome glory that we are changed.

Reading the Word does not only satisfy the soul. It must be meditated and pondered on. It must penetrate our thoughts and minds. It must go deep into our bones and marrows where it is sharp and able to penetrate:

For the word of God is quick, and powerful, and sharper than any two-edged sword, piercing even to the dividing asunder of soul and spirit, and of the joints and marrow, and is a discerner of the thoughts and intents of the heart. (Hebrews 4:12 KJV)

Our blood cells, which are vital for complete function in every part of our bodies, are formed within the bone marrow. When the Word of God enters our marrow, without exception, everything is changed within us…just as it is with our physical bodies and even more with our spiritual bodies. The bone marrow is so essential and powerful that a transplant from a small portion is the cure for many terminal illnesses. The Word of God will change everything, even our spiritual DNA.

As the Prophet beheld the Glory of God, he recognized his sins: "Woe to me!" I cried. "I am ruined! For I am a man of unclean lips, and my eyes have seen the King…" (Isaiah 6:5 KJV). Only vile and doubtful words were spoken from his lip. There is power in our words, whether for good or evil or to produce life or death.

Moses was called and sent by God to speak to Pharoah that the children of Israel might be set free. He too doubted his calling. He responded with negativity just like Isaiah, who also recognized his sinful state and felt doubtful, afraid, and inadequate: "*And the LORD spake unto Moses saying, goo in, speak unto Pharoah king of Egypt, that he let the children of Israel go out of his land. And Moses spake. before the Lord, saying, Behold, the children of Israel have not hearkened unto me; how then shall Pharaoh hear me, who am of uncircumcised lips?*" (Exodus 6:10-12 KJV).

The spirit of discernment is also activated in us as not only do we see our sinful state, but we are made aware of the spiritual structure of our environment, as well as the people around us and the good and evil around us, "*…for mine eyes have seen the King the LORD of Hosts*" (Isaiah 6:5 KJV). We will never leave the presence of the Lord the way we entered. It is such a blessing that the vast and bountiful love and mercy of God deliver us from our sinful state for His purpose and glory. Let us observe the prophet's deliverance in Isaiah 6:6-7 (KJV) "*Then flew one of the seraphims unto me, having a live coal in his hand, which he had taken with the tongs from off the altar: And he laid it upon my mouth, and said, Lo, this hath touched thy lips; and thine iniquity is taken away, and thy sin purged.*"

Here Isaiah was consecrated unto the Lord after he recognized his personal sins, and he confessed them: "*If we confess our sins, he is faithful and just to forgive us our sins, and to cleanse us from all unrighteousness.*" (1 John 1:9 KJV)

The ministry of the burning coals on his lips by the seraphim is symbolic to the sin offering on the alter: "And he laid it upon my mouth, and said, 'Lo this hath touched thy lips; and thine iniquity is taken away, and thy sin purged'" (Isaiah 6:7 KJV). *God* does not call the prepared. He knows each one of us and created us for a purpose. He knows our weaknesses and shortcomings, and as we seek Him, He will reveal Himself to us. It is important for us to seek Him to be cleansed and made whole for His purpose and glory: "For whom he did foreknow, he also did predestinate to be conformed to the image of his Son, that he might be the firstborn among many brethren. Moreover, whom he did predestinate, them he also called: and whom he called, them he also justified: and whom he justified, them he also glorified." *(Romans 8:29-30 KJV).*

Moses and Isaiah also recognized the people around them. They recognized the battles they had to fight. We too must be aware of our surroundings and what must be committed in prayer for us to fulfill the call of God on our lives. All sins, including doubt and unbelief, will hinder us. We also have the enemy who recognizes the call of God on our lives and presents us with attacks and distractions of all sorts because we are surrounded by those unclean spirits, hence the Lord tells us to be separate and come out from among them: *"Therefore come out from among them, and be separate, says the Lord. Do not touch what is unclean, And I will receive you."* (2 Corinthians 6:17 KJV).

This is specifically spoken of a spiritual separation. It may not be physical unless the Lord chooses to do so. When God calls us, we cannot continue in our sinful state, nor can we continue to fellowship with unbelievers. Yes, we must continue to love and pray for them, but the Lord Who has made all things new has called us out. Remember, *"Be not deceived: evil communications corrupt good manners."* (1 Corinthians 15:33 KJV).

God has called each one of us even in our sinful state, which can be a training ground for us. Here we learn to overcome. What we have learned during this time we should use for God's glory and minister to others what we learned in the process. I have repeated this scripture so many times because it speaks so profoundly of the healing we have received and the importance of reaching out to others who are in the place where we have overcome:

"Blessed be God, even the Father of our Lord Jesus Christ, the Father of mercies, and the God of all comfort; Who comforts us in all our tribulation, that we may be able to comfort those who are in any trouble, with the comfort wherewith we ourselves are comforted by God. For as the sufferings of Christ abound in us, so our consolation also aboundeth by Christ." (2 Corinthians 1:3-5 KJV)

As we are changed in His presence, He fills our cleaned and consecrated vessel with His anointing. It is His anointing that breaks every yoke: *"Then he answered and spake unto me, saying, this is the word of the* L\ord *unto Zerubbabel, saying, not by might, nor by power, but by my spirit, saith the* L\ord *of hosts."* (Zechariah 4:6 KJV).

As we respond to the call of God on our lives, I pray we will take time to abide in His Word and in prayer that we will be taught and led by His precious Holy Spirit our teacher, counsellor, and guide.

Pearl 5
The Blueprint:
God's Roadmap for Your Life

Blueprint Poem

My blueprint is established for you each day

So seek Me and pray

With each step, I'll gently lead you through

By My spirit I'll guide and council you

So seek Me, trust Me, and pray

Each step you take with Me, I will gently lead you to My goals for you

This will lead you to life abundantly.

So seek Me, trust Me, and pray

Not alone you will go, for not alone I'll leave you

Oh my child, it is my will that today you seek me and pray

Through your blueprint, I lead you each day

As you seek Me and pray.

Abba Father

It was a quiet Monday morning after seeing my children off to school. I began my household chores when my thoughts were interrupted by the clear voice and unction from the Holy Spirit.

He spoke:

My daughter, when a builder builds a building, he must have sketched, a plan. It is called a blueprint. If he builds without a blueprint, the foundation will not be sturdy and strong. Every wall and the structures of the building will not be properly aligned, and subsequently, everything within the house will also not be properly aligned. The things within will even fall apart due to its poor structure. What about you, my daughter? You are my building, and I have a blueprint for you, my temple in which I reside.

With much curiosity, I asked, "What could be my Blueprint, Lord?" He replied,

Your Blueprint is made up of each day of your life and your daily activities. Like any product that you purchase, there is a manual from the manufacturer when you first open the box. This manual instructs you on how to put the product together so it can operate effectively. Like the manufacturer, I am your Creator and your road map which directs you toward your destiny of living a successful and purposeful life. You must seek me because I am your manual. I am your potter, and you are the clay. I form you into My image and will make you whole. I want you to seek me each day because every day is the blueprint of your life and the roadmap to your destiny. As you seek me daily in prayer and in My Word, this will guide you and be a lamp to your feet and a light to your path.

Abba Father

I am here to remind you that this is not just the call to serve Him, but it also entails our vocation, where to live, whom to marry, what church to attend, whom to serve — every aspect of our lives, with daily activities included. This keeps us in the center of God's will.

This brought me much thought and, yes, even conviction. With much reflection, I wondered:

- How well did I make use of my time and days?
- Were they conducted according to my Father's will, plan, and purpose for my life?
- Did I waste time?

Yes, I was aware of much wasted time of minutes, hours, days, weeks, and years, which resulted in hindrances, derailments, and distractions from God's plan for my life.

Because I was not in alignment with His plans, there were interruptions, and most of my plans fell apart due to the unstable structure and improper blueprint. The Master Builder, the Restorer had to step in and reconstruct my building, my life, and my story.

Sometimes, what we may think to be God's idea is not His idea but our selfish will. It is important to seek the Lord, even as we serve within the Body of Christ. He has given each of His children a task, and it is important for us to be aware of what He has entrusted to us and be obedient and diligent in doing so.

We will not know our calling just by someone prophesying it to us. When such a prophecy is given, if it is indeed God's will, it should bear witness by the Holy Spirit within us, and it also must be a confirmation, because the Lord already revealed that to us. Be aware of false prophecies.

We are led, guided, and instructed each day by the Holy Spirit, who has been given to us to teach, guide, and counsel us. By knowing God's plans and purpose, He will guide us according to His blueprint for our lives. It is therefore important to be sensitive to the leading of the Holy Spirit in our daily activities. Take note of His leading and instructions spoken deep within the recesses of our spirit man. Take note also of the circumstances around us.

I am so aware that He has called me into the ministry of hospitality, mentoring, and caring for others. That's where I got my name, "Mama Pearl." God has gifted me the opportunity to serve his daughters, His "Precious Pearls."

Take note of the things you did or what interested you even from your childhood. These are often indications and preparations for God's plan for your life as explained in my call to be a nurse.

My mother told me that when I disappeared from home, she knew exactly where I was. Yes, I was at the home of the latest baby who was born in the neighborhood. There I helped the mother to take care of her newborn or even helped her with the laundry, which at that time was done by hand. Yes, the seed or vision of being a midwife was planted within me, and this I also pursued. After my studies in England, it was a joy and privilege to return home to Jamaica to serve in the local hospital as a nurse and midwife. I was back to the very place where I conceived the vision and call as I visited, helped, and prayed for the sick during my high school days. I wanted nothing else than to be a nurse.

The desire to help and serve others was built within my DNA. This led me to have deep empathy for others and therefore answer the call to mentor, counsel, and encourage others, something I do even today. This encouraged me to work in mental health for many years. Here I submitted myself to the Holy Spirit to touch the lives of my patients as much as I was able to. I saw many miracles and deliverances as captives were set free from their bondage through God's healing.

As God leads us through His blueprint for our lives, we will experience opened and closed doors. We must not be disappointed about the closed doors because not every door is meant for us to walk through according to God's plan. We will also experience losing friends we may have held dear to our hearts. God saw it fit to remove them because they may have been hindrances on our journey, or they were not prepared to travel with us on the same path.

It was so profound to watch my son Chris, who delighted in building things even from a child. His favorite toys were airplane kits. He took delight in teaching his little brothers how to build these kits. He would sometimes construct large-sized airplanes and use them as decorations in his bedroom. This led to his vocation, which he thoroughly enjoyed and is now retired from. Even to this day, there is hardly anything he cannot build. God truly gifted me with a handy son.

Pay attention to whatever your children or grandchildren show interest in and foster and encourage those seeds in them. It is the seed of their calling. We are to help water their seed with our full support and encouragement. I know of a great pianist who was given a toy piano as a child, and now he has a doctorate in music and is a well-known global pianist.

It is for the Glory of God that we are called to occupy and fill the earth with His glory: *"Who hath saved us, and called us with a holy calling, not according to our works, but according to his own purpose and grace, which was given us in Christ Jesus before the world began."* (2 Timothy 1:9 KJV)

- Abiding in God's work is the key to our Blueprint.

"Thy Word is a lamp to my feet and light to my path."

(Psalm 119:105 KJV)

- It is important to completely trust the Lord for His guidance.

"Trust in the Lord with all thine heart; and lean not unto thine own understanding. In all thy ways acknowledge him, and he shall direct thy paths." (Proverbs 3:5-6 KJV)

God is calling us to be His ambassadors in the earth. We are called to be His hands extended reaching out and ministering to those who are lost and have lost their way and their destiny. Those who are being destroyed by the enemy. Those who have neither joy nor peace and are being tormented every day of their lives. He said, *"The thief cometh not, but for to steal, and to kill, and to destroy; I am come that they might have life, and that they might have it more abundantly."* (John 10:10 KJV)

As we spend time with the Holy Spirit, He will encourage and strengthen us in our calling with His blueprint.

God is calling us to be His hands extended and to reach out to others in love. He wants us to be an expression of His love. There are many hurting souls and those who long for His touch, but they do not know how to come to Him. God wants us to take them into His chamber and let them receive His love. It is within His chambers, the secret place, that His love is released. Bring His beloved children into His chamber and let them feast from the banqueting table of His love, promises, and blessings. They too are hurting, feeble, and weak; so, help those who are feeble and faint-hearted. Let them know there is strength and restoration in our Heavenly Father. The Holy Spirit spoke to my heart in my time of devotion with Him:

My beloved, even as you drink, show them how to drink. Show them how to drink from My refreshing pools, not pools of corruption with every pollutant. Polluted pools make My children sick and feeble. It makes them malnourished in Me. My absolute best is reserved for My beloved children, so help them along the way. Just hold My hand, and as I lead you, you lead them, taking them out of captivity into the peaceful and prosperous place of My abode. Daughter, you have known the pain and trials, the disappointment, the brokenness, and the feeble heartedness of having drunk from polluted pools. Now as you drink from My refreshing pools, give My weary traveler a drink from My refreshing pools; a drink to refresh their soul.

As you feed and feast from My Word, your soul and your spirit are being refreshed, restored, and rejuvenated. My Holy Spirit refreshes your tired soul. Share with others the joy and fellowship of the banqueting table and My springs of refreshing. Drink, My beloved. Drink always. There is always more, and as you come to me, you will never thirst again.

Blessed are you, My child. Now go forth, bearing the fragrance of My love, My blessings, and My truth. Behold I am with you always.

Abba Father

Pearl 6
Disobedience vs Sacrifice

1. What is obedience?
   a. This is an act of doing what we are told to do by law or rule in any given area or situation.
   b. It also means to listen to or pay attention. If applied, it provides positive outcomes, clarity, success, and blessings.
2. Has your disobedience ever cost you?

The Lord requires that we walk in obedience to His Word and His commands. He speaks gently to our hearts, and we should always strive to walk in obedience, which is better than sacrifice.

Obedience is a willingness and readiness to diligently do what we have been asked or instructed to do. The same applies to our relationship with the Lord. His instructions allow us to align ourselves with His plan and purpose for our lives, and it also brings glory to Him. It is a form of worship, and it is therefore important to obey Him in the things He has entrusted to us. There are severe consequences to disobedience. The act of obedience also demonstrates our love and trust in Him, and most importantly, it is a demonstration of the fear of the

Lord.

Obedience ushers His blessings into our lives; it also brings a curse upon us when we disobey Him. We see an example in Jesus' call to suffer and die for us, to redeem us back to God, and to cancel all our sins. What a tremendous blessing! Can we imagine the state of our lives if Jesus did not respond to His Father's instruction to come to earth to die for us? Because of His obedience and our faith in what He did for us, we have eternal life with Him. While on earth, we can enjoy the abundant life He paid the price for. He paid for every sin we have committed and will even unconsciously commit. He said, *"...I come that they may have life, and that they might have it more abundantly."* (John 10:10 KJV).

It is not that everything will be fine while we are on earth, but as we put our trust in Him, we can guarantee that when we face many trials and seek His face in prayer, He will fight all our battles. His obedience to death and having been resurrected gave us the authority to cancel everything that opposes us. If Jesus had disobeyed the call to suffer and die for us, we would have been without hope and would be lost in our sins. He knew the battles that awaited us here on earth and that we were incapable of fighting them. His last words on the cross were, *"It is finished."* (John 19:30 KJV). He then gave victory to all who would believe and trust Him.

Sometimes when God gives us an instruction, it is completely out of our plans or ability to do them. He knows, and He will empower us. However, when we disobey, it robs us of our blessings, and it also takes us away from His plans, purpose, and destiny for our lives.

We do not obey God to be rewarded, but there is a joy that awaits us when we do so. Jesus knew the terrible suffering and shame He had to endure as He chose to obey God to redeem us, but He was willing to do so because He saw the joy that awaited Him. He saw the many souls that would be rescued and delivered from the clutches of the enemy's torment. It may not be easy to do what we have been asked to do and may also cause us some suffering, shame, persecution, and ridicule, but there is also joy and reward that awaits us. (See Hebrews 12:2.) As stated in I Samuel 15:22 (KJV) *"...Behold, to obey is better than sacrifice, and to hearken than the fat of rams."*

The Lord spoke to my heart:

Walking in obedience is the key to fellowship with Me. Being obedient is trusting and loving Me, and it is also walking in the fear of Me, not to be afraid, but honoring and trusting Me. Honoring Me and believing My Word and Who I say I am. Be obedient to My leading and trust Me for every direction and guidance. I guide you according to My plans and purpose for your life, to bring honor and glory to My Name. I lead you away from distractions, so always trust My leading by walking in obedience always. Listen to My still gentle voice. Move by the leading of My Spirit and let My Peace lead and guide you.

Abba Father

My Sacrifice to Obedience

Have you ever found yourself in a place where you had to make a choice of choosing to be obedient contrary to your personal desires or plans?

I found myself in such place when I had no other choice but to leave Chris behind with my parents in order to answer the call to return to England to follow God's plan for my healing and restoration. This was incredibly painful and difficult, as I missed Chris terribly. In as much as I knew he was loved and well cared for by my parents, I felt very guilty leaving him, but this I knew was vital and would be rewarding for both of us, and indeed, it turned out to be so.

It was also a time of great political upheaval in my country, and with previous hurricanes, many basic essentials were not available. I felt very guilty leaving him there during a time when basic resources were scarce nationwide. For that reason, I could not enjoy the luxuries of living in a developed country, as these were not available to him.

I recalled refusing to purchase basic luxury items and things I knew he would enjoy, such as fruits (grapes and apples) and all the essentials a toddler would need. Anything that was not available to him, I could not enjoy. Guilt flooded my heart and, yes, sometimes anger towards myself for having to make that choice of leaving him behind added to the circumstances that caused us to have to return home. This brought me much discomfort as I felt I was robbing him of the care that I needed to give him so early in his life as a mother.

Another time I had to make a sacrifice to be obedient was to decline a wonderful opportunity of completing an 18-month certification to become a registered mental health nurse during my three months of clinical psychiatry studies. Even though this would be an extra credential to my nursing career, I knew this was not God's plan, so I graciously declined.

There are numerous instances of obedience depicted in the Bible, with one of the most prevalent being the instructions for children to obey their parents. This principle holds significant outcomes, either resulting in blessings or curses throughout one's life.

The passage in Ephesians 6:1-3 (KJV) states, "*Children, obey your parents in the Lord, for this is right. Honor your father and mother,*" *which is the first commandment with promise: "that it may be well with thee and thou mayest live long on the earth.*" It emphasizes the importance, and blessings of children obeying their parents in the Lord and honoring them. This commandment holds a promise of a prosperous life and longevity, making it the first commandment with a promise.

I encourage you not to give up on your own healing and restoration journey. Remain steadfast and place your trust in the One who knows the way and holds the answers. Remember that God's presence is with you during difficult times, and He promises to never leave or forsake you. As you cry out to Him and trust in His guidance, He will make a way in your wilderness and illuminate your path with His light. As we choose to obey God's instructions, He will gently and continually lead us.

It is during the most challenging times of our lives, especially when we cry out to the Lord, that we will experience His presence because He loves us so much and will never abandon us in our pain and suffering as long as we look to Him, cry out to Him, and trust Him. I am so thankful that, He is indeed close to the brokenhearted and saves those who are crushed in spirit (See Psalm 34:18).

An example of obedience in the Bible is that of Abram before his name was changed to Abraham. He was told to leave his father's house and go to an unfamiliar place, where God was taking him. God had great plans to prosper him, to make his name great, and to bless him for generations. Sometimes for God to bless us, He may choose to relocate us, as seen in Genesis 12. Those promises remain today for Abraham and his descendants.

I encourage you, my readers, to listen to the still small voice and the nudging of the Holy Spirit. His ways are higher than our ways, and His thoughts are higher than our thoughts. He knows just what we need, and He has the answer. He knows the path and the blueprints for our lives. He is the restorer, and as long as we seek His face, He will lead and guide us in all truth.

Be encouraged and comforted by these words. God is true and faithful to His promises. His glorious name is powerful, yet He has exalted His Word above His mighty name according to Psalm 138:2 (KJV), which states, *"I will worship toward thy holy temple and praise thy Name for thy loving kindness and for thy truth; for thou hast magnified thy Word above all thy name."*

Our ways are not God's ways, and He knows the paths we should go to fulfill His plans and purposes for us. Don't be afraid to follow God's plan and His instructions, especially during difficult times. Trust Him; He will make a way in the wilderness you have found yourself in as long as you seek Him. His faithfulness is sure.

As Isaiah 55:8-9 (NIV) states, *"For my thoughts are not your thoughts, neither are your ways My ways,"* declares the Lord. *"As the heavens are higher than the earth, so are My ways higher than your ways and My thoughts than your thoughts."*

Disobedience brings severe consequences, as seen in the example of Jonah. When God instructs us, it's important not to go the opposite direction. Obedience leads us to our destination and goals. Seek God's help when you make mistakes, and repent.

God instructed Jonah to go to Nineveh, but he chose to go the opposite way out of resentment and disobedience. Disobedience robs us of God's protection and exposes us to the enemy. It also affects the atmosphere around us. Jonah's disobedience caused a great storm, and he admitted his guilt. Similarly, when we disobey God's commands and instructions, it brings storms into our lives, but when we confess and repent, the storms will be calmed, and we will find our way. Jonah was thrown into the sea and swallowed by a great fish as punishment. Confession and repentance lead to calmness and restoration. Remember the lessons from Jonah's story and strive to obey God's instructions to avoid unnecessary storms in your life.

How symbolic is this? Similarly, our Lord Jesus Christ was obedient to suffer and die for us and was buried for three days but rose triumphally from the grave to give us victory, the forgiveness of our sins, and eternal life with Him for all eternity (Matthew 12:40). Just as Jonah was called to go to Nineveh to redeem God's lost people, through our Lord's obedience, we too have been redeemed.

When we find ourselves walking in disobedience, like Jonah, we too should repent and be obedient to what has been entrusted to us. He finally obeyed and went to Nineveh, where he preached to the people. There are some observations to be made here in Jonah 2:1-10 when we disobey God:

- We find ourselves void of God's protection and presence.
- We are transported into a place of unrest, fear, and confusion (i.e., in the belly of Sheol)
- Our troubles are increased, and they continually rage around us.
- There is no peace, nor rest for our souls.

- There is confusion, even as the weeds were wrapped around Jonah's head.

- We become imprisoned and separated, even as Jonah was locked in the belly of the great fish.

  (As Jonah cried out to the Lord and repented, the Lord spoke to the fish, and it vomited him unto the dry land. Like Jonah, when we repent of our disobedience, God will deliver us and place us on the paths destined for us.)

The Importance of Obedience

1. To honor and trust those in authority who have established rules, laws, and regulations for our common good; As we choose to obey God, we honor and trust Him

2. An act of worship to God

3. An expression of our love to Him

4. A demonstration of faith and confidence in God

5. We will be rewarded by God

6. We enjoy a blessed, long, and successful life

7. Disobedience leads to sin, separation from God, and death

<u>Self-Reflection</u>

1. Is there any area in your life God called you to obey Him?

   _____

2. Are you able to identify the call and instruction?

   _____

3. What are your plans to choose the path of obedience and obey the call?

   _____

Prayer

Heavenly Father,

I thank You for saving me through your death on the Cross. I also thank you for Your faithfulness to never leave nor forsake me but to be with me to the very end. You are always with me in every trial, which by Your grace made me stronger.

I answer Your call to follow You and to serve You...to be Your disciple. I thank You for Your instructions given to me, and by Your grace and the help of the Holy Spirit, I choose to obey and honor You.

Please help me to be faithful and to be obedient to Your instructions. Please forgive me when I disobeyed you and was derailed on my journey. I give myself to You so You can use me as Your vessel for your honor and glory.
Thank You, Father. It's in the precious, matchless and powerful Name of Jesus, I pray.

Amen.

As you choose to obey the LORD, He speaks this to your soul:

Showers of Blessings

Showers of blessings, I will pour upon you this day.
Showers of blessings because you seek me and pray and desire to do
My will.

As you journey, I will be with you, you will never be alone. I will always go with you to strengthen you. Always look to Me and seek Me, there you will find comfort, rest, joy, and peace. Trust Me always and be not afraid. Listen for My voice today and obey My commands, there you will experience fullness of joy.

When you do not obey My commands, you grieve My Spirit and My plans for you are hindered. Follow the leading of My Holy Spirit; there you will find rest for your soul. My Spirit causes you to rest. It gives you peace and comfort. Without My Spirit, you are led on the paths of confusion. On My path is peace. Even in the midst of the storm, you will find peace.

Go My child, go in My peace and My strength.
I am with you.

Your Abba Father.

Pearl 7
The Healing

It is God's desire for us all to be healed in every area of our lives, whether it is physical, mental, emotional, or spiritual. For this purpose, Christ Jesus came to earth, suffered, and died on the cross for us who believe in Him. He loves us so much that He does not want to see His beloved children suffer in any area of our lives.

When we experience hurt and pain within, this is called emotional wounding. During this time, bleeding that we cannot visibly see is found deep within us. I heard a speaker once saying as the Holy Spirit revealed to her, "The tears we shed are as blood, and bleeding takes place within us."

We see that of our Lord Jesus Christ. While in agony of the cruel punishment and death on the cross and what awaited Him, He experienced so much stress as He prayed, *"... that His sweat was as it were great drops of blood falling to the ground."* (Luke 22:44 KJV)

Likewise, when we too are stressed beyond measure through the brokenness of our soul, there is bleeding within that we cannot see with the naked eye. This brokenness comes through different forms of abuses, the main one being words that are like poisonous arrows, piercing our soul. Proverbs 12:18 (NIV) states, *"The words of the reckless pierce like swords, but the tongue of the wise brings healing."* It is much easier to take care of a physical wound and observe it's healing, but we cannot see an emotional wound. We can only recognize it by the deep pain and sorrow we feel within.

Emotional wounds are caused by human experiences that cause deep pain and anguish of the soul to a psychological level, which can be inflicted by anyone and most often those who are dear and close to us. The closer the relationship and trust we have in the individual, the deeper the pain, due to the depth of acceptance and closeness of the relationship, through the knitting of our souls. When a separation occurs through a betrayal or divorce, our souls are literally ripped, and there the bleeding takes place. Healing becomes difficult due to the fragmentation of the wounded soul.

It may be a spouse, parents, siblings, friends, or colleagues. This is classified as the wounding of one's spirit. This woundedness, if remained untreated and unhealed, causes various mental, psychological, and physical disorders which often leads to surgical interventions and various malignant illnesses, such as cancer. This is also the outcome of generational curses. If we sincerely love our children, let's choose to break this cycle.

I encourage you today by letting you know that we are so special to God and that our woundedness has not gone unnoticed by Him. His eyes are always on us, and He sees deep within the recesses of our souls when and where we are hurting, and He is always available to bring healing to us.

The Wounded Spirit

Definition: A wounded spirit is a brokenness, laceration, and fragmentation of the soul.

The brokenness of the vital essence and foundations of the inner man is essential for character development and living a successful life. It can also be described as an enslaved or imprisoned soul. This can occur at any stage of one's life:

- psychological wounds that affect our relationships and acts of daily life
- wounded brokenness, laceration, a spirit that is broken and shattered
- the brokenness of the vital essence of the inner man
- shattered foundations for essential living and character development
- an enslaved or imprisoned soul
- many painful and frustrating situations
- others blamed for one's feelings

Most things in life are perceived as stressful situations because of the inability to cope. We have problems dealing or interacting with most people around us, no matter the environment. It may be within the home with parents and siblings, in the workplace, or in our marriages. Everything is perceived as being negative and stressful.

Stages of Woundedness

Infancy Stage:

A spirit of rejection (A dart of the enemy); this occurs in utero due to the following:

- Single parenting or unwanted pregnancy
- Divorce, separation, marital problems, or drunkenness
- Sexual preferences, such as in Eastern countries
- Poor bonding during infancy; infant not held and caressed and loved during early years
- No communication and parental interaction during the early years
- Adoption, abandonment, planned abortion
- Hearing and witnessing fights, conflicts, and arguments in the home

Pre-school Stage:

- Children experience all the above from the infancy stage; experience pain but cannot explain the reason or how they feel
- Guilty — blame themselves and feel responsible
- Experience many accidents and illnesses
- Psychological and Physical growth delays
- Develop mistrust
- Always needy of attention from important people in their lives, such as parents, family members, teachers, pastors, or special friends
- Psychosocial problems, such as lying, stealing, conflicts with friends, fighting, and always seeking attention to self
- Tension
- Bedwetting
- Desiring some sort of self-stimulation
- Banging head
- Biting nails
- Stuttering
- Carries a blanket or special toy for comfort

Preadolescence Stage:

- Shattered lives
- Low self-esteem and self-worth
- Sexual promiscuity
- Instabilities in various aspects of their lives, especially at school and their communities
- Problems with the law
- Repeated and deliberate misbehavior
- Lack of respect for authority
- Always striving to please others or to be accepted by others
- Withdrawal, isolation, depression, and sometimes suicide
- Competitiveness
- Lack of decision-making
- Hurts self or others
- Puts self or others down; name calling, judgmental, blames others for mistakes, and finds excuses to justify behavior
- Physical characteristics — sad affect, poor eye contact, dull appearance

Adult Stage:

- All the above
- Death, Separation, Divorce

Foundational Prevention for Children:

- Always establish communication, thus encouraging expression of thoughts and feelings.

- Provide a warm loving and secure environment.

- Know who we are in Christ Jesus. We have been redeemed from the curse and snares of the enemy.

- Discipline appropriately as needed.

- Always allow our children to feel that they are important and valuable to us.

- Respect them and their feelings.

- Give direction in the choice of friends they keep.

- Compliment them; speak things into being as though they were even though they are not.

- Encourage and foster forgiveness. Ask for their forgiveness.

- Encourage them to develop interesting skills.

- Tap into and encourage their gifts and callings. This will counteract any weaknesses and help to capitalize on their strengths. It also prevents them from being idle, thus leaving room for the enemy.

- Allow our lives to be an example to our children.

- Pay attention to peer and neighborhood pressure.

- Listen and support.

- Find the root cause for any unusual situation.
- Use maternal instincts.

- Teach your children the Word of God for any situation.

If all these fundamental situations are not dealt with early on in their lives, they continue into adulthood and become worse, including the following:

- Increasing inadequacies and failures
- More difficult to deal with
- Others around are affected

Woundedness prevents one from walking in victory, always feeling defeated and hopeless, and inferior:

- We are subject to all sorts of illnesses and diseases due to stress.
- We cannot receive love.
- We cannot radiate God's love.
- We cannot hear God's voice.
- We are more in tune with the spirit that has enslaved us…the spirit of darkness.

<u>Scriptures on Woundedness</u>

Proverbs 17:22 (KJV) "A merry heart does good like medicine, but a broken spirit dries the bones."

Proverbs 15:13 (KJV) "A merry heart makes a cheerful countenance, but by sorrow of the heart the spirit is broken.

Proverbs 18:14 (KJV) "The Spirit of a man will sustain his infirmity, but a wounded spirit who can bear?"

Isaiah 53
Hebrews 4:15-16 (KJV) *"For we do not have a High Priest who cannot sympathize with our weaknesses, but was in all points tempted as we are, yet without sin."*

Jesus suffered rejection but overcame that we too could overcome. He saw what was beyond the suffering: *"Looking unto Jesus the author and finisher of our faith; who for the joy that was set before Him endured the cross, despising the shame, and is set down at the right hand oof the throne of God."* (Hebrews 12:2 KJV).

1 Samuel 1:10 (KJV) *"And she was in bitterness of soul and prayed unto the Lord and wept sore."*

Hannah was sad and broken because her rival, Peninnah, mocked and teased her year after year because of her barrenness. While praying in the temple in Shiloh, Eli the priest accused her of being drunk. She did not give up. The Lord blessed her. The main cause of brokenness is rejection.

Major Bondages to be healed from:

- Low self-esteem
- Negative of pessimistic thinking
- Guilt, anger, fear, doubt, and unbelief
- Grief and disappointment
- Unforgiveness
- Occult involvement
- Addictive behavior
- Illicit sexual activity
- Rejection and shame
- Negative influences
- The aftermath of any abuse.

Outcomes of Emotional Wounds

- A feeling that accompanies hopelessness and low self-esteem.
- Inability to cope with life and life's circumstances.
- Unstable or poor relationships.
- Inability to make decisions.
- Inability to accept or see ourselves the way God sees us
- Inability to give or receive love
- Prevents us from achieving our goals in life or fulfilling our destiny
- Paralyzes or immobilizes us
- The feeling of betrayal, rejection, and abandonment
- Shame, unworthiness, and guilt

- Anger, resentment, and bitterness

- Fear

- Rebellion

- Confusion and the inability to make decisive decisions

- Insecurity

- Various addictions, such as food, alcohol, tobacco, drugs, shopping, TV, movies, sports, sexual addictions, and pornography. There is also the desire to escape through anorexia nervosa and bulimia nervosa. This involves eating and purging through vomiting or using laxatives, which is evidenced through weight loss and general poor health.

Fruits of Rejection and Brokenness:

- Disillusionment, doubt, fear, and mistrust

- Isolation, anger, bitterness, and jealousy

- Depression, negativism, lack of control, and confidence

- Hostility, rebellion, self-pity, disobedience, and disrespect

- Sexual promiscuity, various addictions of all sorts, and codependency

Compare with the fruits of the spirit — the Word of God sown versus the bad seed of rejection. People who are wounded have difficulty walking in the fruits of the Spirit or having a successful Spirit-filled life. These are love, joy, peace, long-suffering, kindness, goodness, faithfulness, gentleness, and self-control, according to Galatians 5:22-23.

God wants to see us whole in our bodies and in our minds. *"Beloved, I wish above all things that thou mayest prosper and be in health, even as thy soul prospereth."* (3 John 1:2 (KJV)

James 5:14-15 speaks not only of healing the body, but the soul as well. Rejection is a bad seed that is planted in our spirit. It brings forth a bad tree and bad fruits. God intends for us to be trees of righteousness. He desires for us to be His beautiful trees of righteousness planted by His river of life, and His Holy Spirit is available to bring forth healing and deliverance to us.

As mentioned in Isaiah 61:3 (KJV), *"To appoint unto them that mourn in ion, to give unto them beauty for ashes, the oil of joy for mourning, the garment of praise for the spirit of heaviness; that they might be called trees of righteousness, the planting of the LORD, that he might be glorified."*

Prayer

Heavenly Father,

I thank You for loving me by sending your only begotten Son, our Lord Jesus Christ, to set me free from all that is contrary to Your will for my life.

I ask You Heavenly Father to search my innermost being and remove every pain and sorrow deep within the recesses of my soul concerning_____ (offender's name(s)_____. I choose to release to you and completely choose to receive Your healing, in the Name of Jesus.

I forgive and release all those who have caused me deep pain and woundedness, and I thank you that by the stripes of the Lord Jesus Christ, I am healed.

I forgive_____for causing me pain. I commit myself to Your care. In the mighty and matchless name of Jesus Christ of Nazareth. Amen

Pearl 8
Choosing Your Purpose Partner

Choosing the right partner is very important. We should be mindful and prayerful of God's partner for us. Do not get caught up and committed to your expectations of what you'd like your partner to become instead of who they truly are. When people show you who they are, believe them.

I can speak from my own personal experience trying not to be caught up, as we must never assume that when situations are presented to us it is always God-ordained. We may see a particular pattern and think *This has to be God*, as we perceive them to be signs of God's approval with what seems to be coincidences, thus believing the relationship is God-ordained. We must be led by His peace.

When people see someone they like, they admire them because they're caught up in the temporary fireworks. They admire you because you stand out, and you're a convenience until the fireworks wear off. Take notes of the **'RED FLAGS,'** which tend to show up when we do not lead with God's peace. This is a big warning sign which should not be ignored. We are not men's mothers, whose job it is to raise and train them into becoming responsible men.

When I met my ex, I had just then ended a three-year courtship that I thought was indeed God-ordained because we met through a very close friend (who became a sister to me) only about three months after arriving in England. They had known each other from home, and he was like a brother to her. The strange coincidence and what seemed to be God-ordained events that blindsided me was that I met him one day before his birthday, and the following day was my birthday. Because these are rare occurrences, I thought this was such a great coincidence and meant to be, until the true person manifested himself. The lesson behind this is to never assume. The enemy is very cunning. He monitors, imitates God, and tries to derail us.

Young and naïve, this relationship was not without much heartache and mistrust. With his sister's encouragement, after three years of dating, I ended the relationship. Today after over 55 years, she remains one of my closest friends. Thank you, Bev.

I told my ex about this, how disappointed and hurt I was, and how hesitant I was to trust anyone again. He promised he would never hurt me and expressed much understanding. He would always make a note on the envelope of his many letters from overseas, reminding me he would never hurt or disappoint me. How convincing and how disappointing and painful this new-founded relationship turned out to be.

I saw what I thought to be admirable qualities in him. He was handsome, well-mannered, and appeared very caring, with promises to love and care always. I thought this was God's plan of restoration for me.

We must be wise and not be blinded by how someone initially presents themselves in a good light, leading us to assume it is always God-ordained It is only by seeking the Lord in prayer that this will be confirmed. This can be very presumptuous when we have no knowledge of the individual's lifestyle or the family's background. I share this as a caution to everyone. It can be very disastrous to go into a relationship without giving it much thought or praying about it. The enemy plans and orchestrates meetings, places, connections, or circumstances to introduce us to the wrong person, his evil choice. This is a quite common occurrence. It is also a very good example of what will eventually lead to an unhealthy soul tie. Here we lose identity and confidence in ourselves and end up being distracted by the wrong partner.

God has a plan for each of His children and the enemy constantly observes us through monitoring spirits to hinder this. We must therefore be very diligent and prayerful in everything. As stated in 1 Peter 5:8 (KJV), we must be, *"sober, be vigilant; because your adversary the devil walks about like a roaring lion, seeking whom he may devour."*

Choosing The Right Partner

In our quest for a life partner, we look for certain qualities in each other. There are different factors that attract us to each other. I have observed that, in some cases, many see qualities in the individual and pretend to be sincere, loving, and caring only to be trapped by their endearments. After a while, their true colors come out, and they are proven to be what they are not. Only by God's grace can such a marriage survive. There are times when the individual must stand their ground to maintain their identity, who they are, and who they were perceived to be.

We must not allow people in their weaknesses and quest for a good spouse to rob us of who we are or who we are meant to become. It is therefore only too obvious that we are dealing with a very opportunistic individual who wants what he or she sees but is not qualified nor equipped to truly embrace and cherish what they have been presented with. Those qualities are not in them, and this is where various types of abuses are manifested, due to a lack of respect, love, truth, commitment, and appreciation. Again, when people show truly who they are, believe them. Do not abuse their kindness and their gentleness or whatever good and admirable qualities we see in them. Continue to respect and cherish them and recognize your blessings. In such an occurrence, the Bible tells us that we are not to be unequally yoked: *"Be not unequally yoked together with unbelievers: for what fellowship hath righteousness with unrighteousness: and what communion hath light with darkness?"* (2 Corinthians 6:14 KJV)

Coming from a small community in my homeland, much emphasis was placed on choosing the right partner. Everyone knew each other, and if we did not know the individual from another community who was not favorable, somehow, we would learn about them from people who knew them, and pursuing a relationship with that person would then be discouraged or encouraged. We also see the caution and importance of arranged marriages in many cultures. These too are not without problems, as no one is perfect.

God loves us; therefore, He has a plan and order to connect His people. He does not desire for us to be unequally yoked. Just because one goes to church does not mean they are following the Lord. I have known of situations where the spouse and most often the husband puts on a front by attending church (as was in my situation) during their courting days, then after the wedding, that completely changed. I was told of one situation where the wife was told by her husband that he did what she wanted him to do, but he had no further plans to continue. What the wife wanted was a man who loved and served the Lord. For a while, he pretended to be everything she wanted. She reminded him of the importance of working out his own salvation according to the scriptures, as stated in Philippians 2:12 (KJV), *"Wherefore, my beloved, as ye have always obeyed, not as in my presence only, but much more in my absence, work out your own salvation with fear and trembling."*

Thank God for His promises*: "For the unbelieving husband is sanctified by the wife and the unbelieving wife is sanctified by the husband: else were your children unclean, but now are they holy."* (1 Corinthians 7:14 KJV)

It is such a blessing to have a strong Christ-centered relationship between husband and wife. It brings stability and growth in the relationship. It creates a bond of unity with the commanded promise of God's blessing according to Psalm 133. The inability to stand together in prayer and unity creates an open door for the enemy, and the outcome is discord and unfruitfulness. It not only affects our relationship, but also our children.

I recall my precious and godly mother-in-law's counsel on my wedding day — "A family that prays together stays together." I admire the faith of one of my English moms who loved the Lord and faithfully served Him. She prayed for her unbelieving husband for twenty years; she never gave up on him. He later gave his life to the Lord, whom their entire large family ended up serving. Their daughters married spouses who became pastors as well as their children, who became pastors, and the entire family is serving the Lord. This is an example of what can result from a faithful praying wife.

When one is not born of the Spirit of God, he or she has the old adamic nature, a spirit that is unregenerated and full of darkness and carries over into relationships. As believers in the Lord Jesus Christ, we should seek and trust the Lord to bring us His sons and daughters who are of the household of faith with a born-again spirit, which is regenerated and bears the characteristics of our Lord Jesus Christ.

I like Ephesians 5:6 (KJV) which tells us, *"Let no man deceive you with vain words; for because of these things cometh the wrath of God upon the children of disobedience."* God desires to bless us in every area of our lives, so we should not be enticed or carried away with vain words nor imaginations in believing what seems to be of God when it is not.

We are called and appointed to establish God's will on the earth by glorifying Him with our lives and replenishing the earth. Both husband and wife have their role in this. We are to build families which will eventually glorify God.

Please see Ephesians 5:25-33. The husband is instructed to love his wife as Christ loves the church and for which He gave His life. It broke my heart to hear of a young wife who said, "If my husband should see me on fire, he would not even throw a cup of water on me to put the fire out." My heart truly bled for the depravity of such a lost and empty soul who lacks love and empathy and desires the worst for the woman he made a covenant with, in the presence of God, to love and cherish until death separates them. We must remember that we will all stand before God to give account for all our actions.

The fact of the matter is, we truly treat each other according to our relationship with God. If the fear of God is in us, we will do what is right before Him. We must not deceive ourselves. Our thoughts and actions are not hidden from God.

The relationship between husband and wife is very similar to that of Christ and the church — His Bride. Please note that this is very important, as scripture says. One cannot truly and sincerely love God and hate his brother or sister, as "Whoever claims to love God yet hates a brother or sister is a liar. For whoever does not love their brother and sister, whom they have seen, cannot love God, whom they have not seen." (1 John 4:20 NIV)

The wife has her role and responsibility also as is described in Proverbs 31:10-31 (KJV). An excerpt of this scripture is as follows:

- v10-12 "Who can find a virtuous woman? For her price is far above rubies.
- v11 "The heart of her husband doth safely trust in her, so he shall have no need of spoil."
- v12 "She will do him good and not evil all the days of her life."

The rest of the passage gives a full "job description." This is not only for Mother's Day but all the days of her life as she nurtures a Godly home and atmosphere for her husband and children, thus glorifying God and making their home a glorious habitation for the Holy Spirit to dwell in.

Personal Reflection

As you read this book, I encourage you to look at your relationship with your spouse and honestly ask yourself if it represents the love and fear of the Almighty God whom you serve. Nothing is hidden from Him, and again, remember that one day we will have to stand before Him to give an account for our actions. Is the Lord honored in your relationship?

If you have found yourself lacking, confess this to Him. He is gracious enough to forgive and bring restoration to your relationship, as referenced in 1 John 1:9 (NIV): *"If we confess our sins, He is faithful and just and will forgive us our sins and purify us from all unrighteousness."*

As we surrender and seek His face to lead, guide, and teach us, He will send His precious Holy Spirit to teach us all that we need to learn. According to John 14:26 (KJV), *"But the Comforter, which is the Holy Spirit, whom the Father will send in My Name, He shall teach you all things, and bring all things to your remembrance, whatsoever I have said to you."*

Everything we need to know will be taught to us by the Holy Spirit, not just in our relationship, but in every aspect and expectation in our lives, our family, and our home. Sometimes it means, as scripture tells us, to "die to self" in Romans 6:6 (KJV): *"Knowing this, that our old man is crucified with him, that the body of sin might be destroyed, that henceforth we should not serve sin."*

1. From 1-10, how satisfied are you with your marriage or relationship (with 10 being the most satisfied)?

   _____

2. What can you do to show your spouse that you are sincerely devoted and cherish your relationship?

   _____

3. What adjustments or changes can you make to improve your relationship?

   _____

4. Is there an area in your life where you need to die to self to improve your relationship?

   _____

5. Do you know your spouse's likes and dislikes or what makes him/her happy?

   _____

6. Do you feel your partner is equipped to be your purpose partner?

   _____

7. Do you know you and your partner's love languages?

   _____

Prayer
For the Married Person

Heavenly Father,

I thank You for my marriage. I invite you to be Lord of our lives and home as we surrender to you.

I thank You that You formed us into Your own image to love each other as You love us. I ask you to help me to love my spouse as you desire me to love, bringing you glory and honor. I ask you to help me with my weaknesses where I fail to love and serve as I should.

I pray for increased sensitivity to serve as I am required to serve as I die to self.

I ask you to bless my spouse. Please help me to support him/her in all that matters to him/her and to daily encourage and bless him/her.

I pray for increased sensitivity to serve as I am required to serve as I die to self.

I pray for Your blessings and directions in all that we do as a couple. Please bless our lives, our family, our home, and all that concerns us.

I surrender myself to you in service and to my marriage.

In Jesus' mighty name, I pray,

Amen

Prayer

<u>For the Single Person</u>

Heavenly Father,

I thank you for the love, plans, and purposes you have for my life.

I ask you to please lead me by you Holy Spirit to the spouse you have prepared for me.

I commit myself to you as you prepare me for marriage, and I ask you to prepare my spouse.

Please help me to know by the leading of Your Holy Spirit when I meet that person and help me to be led by your peace and not by vain imaginations. I ask for a spouse who loves you first before he/she loves me.

I thank You for your preparation, Your leading to the person of Your choosing, and Your blessing on the relationship.

In the mighty and precious Name of Jesus Christ of Nazareth, I pray,

Amen.

Pearl 9
Soul Ties

What is a Soul Tie?

It is the knitting or cleaving of one's soul like a magnet to someone else, thus becoming one flesh. Both individuals are connected in a very strong and inseparable way. This knitting is done in the spirit realm, and it can either be good or bad. In a marriage relationship, as the pastor declares, "you are now one flesh;" both souls are now in a covenant relationship under God's covenant blessing.

Outside of a marriage relationship where there may be the presence of weaknesses, insecurity, mistrust, disloyalty, and every unhealthy behavior and instability in the relationship, the soul becomes fragile, fragmented, and wounded. This is a bad soul tie.

A soul tie can also be described as a deep and intense connection between two people that goes beyond the physical or the superficial. It is a bond that is formed on a spiritual and emotional level and can be difficult to break, even after the relationship has ended, because of its tightly bonded connection. Our soul is a very essential part of our makeup. We are a tripartite being of soul, spirit, and body. Our spirit and soul are housed within our bodies. The soul is the seat of our memory. It controls the very essence of our lives, feelings, convictions, imaginations, behaviors, and affections. There is great value to our soul according to Mark 8:35-36. It is therefore very important to pay attention in choosing a partner with whom we can have a healthy bonded and trusted relationship, not one that is connected by the temporary satisfactions of life or governed by our emotions, but one that is committed to love, nurture, and care for each other as we grow and prosper together.

The book of 3 John 1:2 (KJV) tells us, *"Beloved, I wish above all things that you mayest prosper and be in health, even as thy soul prospereth."*

Soul ties can be developed in a variety of relationships, including romantic partnerships, friendships, and family relationships. They can be positive (providing a sense of love, support, and understanding) or negative, (resulting in feelings of being overly attached and co-dependent, causing emotional pain).

Positive soul ties can be a source of strength and comfort, providing a sense of belonging and connection to another person. Negative soul ties, on the other hand, can be toxic, draining, and destructive, leaving individuals feeling trapped and unable to move on from unhealthy relationships. Because of the fragmentation of the soul in an unhealthy relationship, the pattern of continued destructive behavior, one unproductive relationship after another, continues unless that damaged soul is healed.

In this very strong relationship where there is a very strong bond between the two individuals, there is the reality of a somewhat forced or obligated commitment to each other. Again, this can be good or bad. It allows the building up and growth of the individuals, whereas in a bad way, it can be very destructive by causing:

- a state of confusion with loss of peace in our lives. There always seem to be problems in the relationship with many unpredicted and unresolved problems, always feeling pressured, accused, and blamed for unknown situations.
- the inability to think clearly or function effectively, due to many conflicts.
- feelings of being controlled or imprisoned.
- loss of individuality, identity, and self-confidence.
- lack of independence, liberty, and personal freedom.
- lack of ability to live up to one's expectations, ability, and goals.
- hindrances in one's spiritual growth and hindrance in trusting our Heavenly Father. This can be very detrimental.
- feelings of being enslaved to the relationship.
- feelings of being compromised or manipulated and misunderstood.

- loss of good health.
- derailment of God's plans for our lives.

There are many diseases that are the outcome of the emotional dysfunctions associated with a bad soul tie. One can be affected by mental disorders such as depression, anxiety, fear, and insomnia.

Some of the physical ailments include high blood pressure, headaches, migraines, heart failure, and stroke. Very common ones are autoimmune diseases, irritable bowel syndrome, arthritis, ulcerative colitis, Crohn's disease, and cancer, to name a few. It is therefore very important to pay attention to our emotional and mental health and not allow ourselves to be controlled or abused in a toxic soul-tie relationship.

What Causes Soul Ties?

A soul tie is a God-given gift because He desires to create a healthy bond between two individuals as we grow and prosper together. God created Adam and then created Eve for Adam because He said it was not good for man to be alone: *"And the Lord God said, it is not good that the man should be alone; I will make him an help meet for him."* (Genesis 2:18 KJV).

It shows here that they both needed each other; they were created to help each other. She was created to help him in every area of his life, that is mentally, emotionally, physically, and spiritually. These are the entities of a good relationship that seals it for growth, development, and productivity. Both the souls of Adam and Eve were knitted together.

A soul tie can be created through emotional attachment and dependency, as individuals become deeply invested in the emotional well-being and happiness of each other. This can happen in any type of relationship, not just romantic.

It is important to be cautious of having unhealthy soul ties, especially soul tie prematurely before marriage through sexual intercourse. In an intimate relationship, the two individuals become one, which is a representation of being spiritually married.

One potential danger of forming a soul tie through sexual activity before marriage is that it can create an emotional bond that can be difficult to break if the relationship is unhealthy, not meant to be, or not meant to last. It can be very destructive to oneself if it is not under the sanctity of God's covenant blessings and approval. When the relationship becomes unhealthy, it is difficult to break away, thus causing much pain, regret, and unrest in the soul. It is here that one's spirit becomes broken and damaged through much emotional pain. This can also affect one's health with different mental health issues.

Having a soul tie in an unhealthy relationship makes it ten times harder to break free from this bondage and trauma because your souls are tied together on a deeper spiritual and intimate level, which can make you spiritually blind. It can be emotionally and spiritually paralyzing, as it hinders progress and the achievement of one's goals in life.

A bad soul tie causes you to feel stuck in the relationship for all the wrong reasons due to fear of letting go or starting over. Soul ties can create a deep sense of attachment and spiritual connection that can be difficult to break, even if the relationship is toxic or abusive. It is quite like having a divorce.

When individuals have a soul tie with someone, it can create a sense of shared energy and emotional baggage, making it harder to move on from negative patterns of behavior or emotional trauma. This can result in feelings of entrapment, helplessness, and confusion, as individuals struggle to break free from the emotional and spiritual bonds that exist between them and their partner. It causes one to lose one's autonomy, which is the inability to think or act for oneself.

How a Soul Tie is Formed

1.   **Sexual Intercourse**

A soul tie is formed after you have had a sexual relationship with a person.

From a medical perspective, oxytocin is released, and this hormone plays a significant part in establishing a strong emotional bond between both partners, thus forming a spiritual connection to a very deep and inseparable level.

For this reason, it is important to pay attention to our emotions and the effect they can have on us permanently, whether for good or bad. When one engages in the act of sex before marriage, it either knits the individuals together or rips their souls apart. God's order for this is to wait until He has blessed and sanctified our covenant relationship. Without His blessings, there is an open door for the enemy to steal, kill, and destroy, as is his job description.

2.   **Close Relationships with a Person**

When we spend a long time in a deep relationship with a person, a soul tie can be created through emotional bonding.

3.   **Involuntary Attachment**

This occurs in human production where the mother is emotionally connected to the unborn child. The infant is involuntarily connected and totally dependent on its mother for life, nourishment, oxygen, and blood supply.

The mother passes on the child's DNA which determines the characteristics of the child, which includes things such as the color of hair, eyes, and skin, as well as the height and structure of the child.

In some situations, the mother's DNA, addictions such as alcoholism, drug addiction, or any other type of behavior may be transferred through the blood system in the umbilical cord, by which the child is attached to the mother.

Today, bonding with the mother is encouraged immediately after birth, whereby the baby is placed skin-to-skin with its mother for close contact. If the mother chooses to breastfeed her baby, this is also done immediately after birth. This is a very healthy form of bonding for mother and baby.

It is also very important for the mother to be rested, and much support is given as she recuperates in order to nurture her baby and establish proper bonding.

1. **Voluntary Attachment**

This occurs after birth when mother and baby are bonded where; trust, love, confidence, and security are established. There have been situations when a child may have developed insecurity, mistrust, lack of confidence, and unhealthy growth process due to no bonding after birth.

Bonding is also very important with the father after birth. I have observed disruptive behaviors in various ways in individuals where this was missing, which was manifested even in one's adult life and behaviors.

How to Recognize That You Have a Soul Tie with Someone

1. You feel an emotional bond and deep connection with the individual, and you always long to spend endless time with them. This could be spiritual or emotional.

2. You are always thinking of the individual and could be obsessed with them always wanting to be a part of their lives and constantly wanting to do things together and sometimes fantasizing about them.

3. The individual seems to always show up just when you need them and is always willing to go above and beyond to help, or vice versa.

4. They occupy your thoughts constantly, which can be overwhelming.

5. You yearn for their approval and find it impossible to make an important decision without their input.

6. There is a false belief and assumption that this person was brought into your life for a purpose, thus making it difficult to let go.

7. You begin to lose understanding and acceptance of yourself and that you must fit into that person's mold.

8. There is much pressure to meet their standards or expectations.

9. You are stuck in their expectations of you.

10. When the relationship is broken, it causes much woundedness, stagnation, and inability to move on.

Breaking free from an unhealthy relationship and breaking the soul tie can be a difficult and painful process that requires emotional healing, self-reflection, and support from trusted friends or professionals. However, it is important to recognize that breaking the soul tie and moving on from toxic relationships can lead to emotional freedom, healing, and growth.

In John 4:16-19, Jesus spoke to the woman at the well about her five husbands she had soul ties with, yet none of them was her actual husband. They were indeed her spiritual husbands but not in a covenant relationship. Throughout their conversation, Jesus showed the woman deep compassion, empathy, and understanding despite her past mistakes and sinful living situation with the history of these five men. He offered her spiritual healing and a relationship with Him and brought healing to her for her habitual soul ties. I am sensing here that Jesus saw a woman who was broken and fragmented because of what was transferred to her through her many uncovenanted sexual contacts. Much is transferred from one individual to another during a sexual relationship, and this can be very detrimental to one's soul in a bad soul tie. He saw a captive woman whom He had to deliver and set free as applied to His call and mission in Isaiah 61.

There is no better intimacy than having a deep connection with Christ Jesus, which goes beyond the physical or emotional intimacy we crave with others.

How to Receive Healing from Soul Ties

To break negative soul ties from a toxic relationship, we should first recognize and acknowledge the situation we are in. The first step is to forgive the individual and forgive ourselves. Here we not only release ourselves from the imprisonment, but we also release them from their established imprisonment. We will need to engage in emotional healing and self-care practices such as prayers, repentance, application of God's Word, deliverance, and counseling. It is important to recognize that breaking a soul tie can be a difficult and painful process, but it is necessary to achieve emotional healing and freedom for one's mental and physical health.

There may be situations, as I personally experienced, where you have to repent for having gone against God's will and plans for your life and totally commit yourself to Him for healing. Sometimes we see the signs, as the Holy Spirit Himself reveals them to us, yet we pursue the relationship or choose to remain in it once it has been manifested. We therefore must repent, which was the first stage of my healing.

Remember the scripture in 1 John 1:9 (NIV), *"If we confess our sins, he is faithful and just and will forgive us our sins and purify us from all unrighteousness."* More specifically, we must:

1. Recognize the situation we are in.

2. Accept that the relationship is over.

3. Forgive the individual and yourself.

4. Spend quiet time for prayer, personal growth, and counseling as needed.

5. Do not rush into a new relationship and allow time for proper healing.

Prayer in Breaking Unhealthy Soul Ties

Father,

It's in the Name of Jesus I repent of my involvement in any unhealthy relationship(s).

Please forgive me for not having sought You, trusted, or obeyed You in my relationship(s).

I forgive _____ for all the hurt, betrayal, and disappointments.

I sever and cut off all influence and connection from_____ _____ in Jesus's Mighty name.

I choose to return anything that connects or reminds me of _ _____.

I reclaim all that I have lost, and I wash myself in the Blood of Jesus.

I commit and surrender myself to you. Thank you for healing me in Jesus's mighty name.

Amen.

Pearl 10
Soulmate

The opposite of soul tie is having a soul mate. This is having a healthy and productive relationship with a person with whom we are destined to experience deep, natural, and healthy feelings and connections.

This relationship is governed and controlled by love, trust, respect, loyalty, and honor. This person was chosen by God to be connected to us as we form a common bond in growing and complementing each other. He or she is God's perfect match, whom He has designed to complement and complete our lives to fulfill His plans and purposes for our lives. Our souls are connected to each other in ways that go beyond physical or emotional attraction. The relationship is usually sealed with a promise as is seen in a marriage covenant, "until death do us part." A soulmate is a good source of spiritual and emotional growth and fruitfulness in one's life. This also honors God.

A typical example of a soul mate is seen in the book of Genesis. When God created Eve as a companion for Adam, he said, *"It is not good for the man to be alone. I will make a help meet for him."* (Genesis

2:18 KJV). God has a soul mate for every one of us as our purpose and life partner.

Throughout the Bible, there are numerous examples of people finding suitable partners or spouses, such as Isaac and Rebekah, Ruth and Boaz, and Joseph and Mary. These relationships were built on a foundation of love, respect, and commitment, which were chosen and blessed by God.

In the New Testament, the Apostle Paul provides guidance on marriage and relationships, emphasizing the importance of mutual respect and selflessness. He encourages couples to love and honor each other and to submit to one another out of reverence for Christ (see Ephesians 5:21-33). Remember that Christ loves us as He loves the church. A marital relationship is like our relationship with the Lord because we are His bride.

While the Bible does not specifically use the term "soul mate," it does provide guidance and wisdom for building strong, healthy relationships with the right and suitable partner. It encourages us to seek out companions who share our values, faith, beliefs, and goals, and to build relationships based on love, respect, trust, and commitment. Ultimately, the Bible teaches us that relationships should bring us closer to God and help us grow in our faith and love for Him, just as we should in our personal and marital relationships.

According to the concept of soul mates, this connection is so strong that it can withstand the test of time, distance, and any obstacles that come our way. It is the idea that this person is the missing piece of our puzzle and that we can only truly be happy and fulfilled when we are with our soul mate. It is about finding someone who understands us in a way that no one else can and who makes us feel whole and complete as we protect and care for each other.

However, it is important to remember that finding a soul mate is not just about finding someone who completes us but most importantly who compliments us and is compatible as we serve with devotion to each other. It is also about building a strong, healthy relationship based on mutual respect, love, and understanding. It takes work and commitment to build a lasting partnership with our soul mate, but the rewards can be immeasurable. It makes us one in the spirit, with God being in the center bonding us together.

How to Recognize the Right Soul Mate

In the book 2 Corinthians 6:14-18 (KJV), we are told not to be unequally yoked with unbelievers. We recognize our soul mate through the evidence of personal similar likes and dislikes, faith, beliefs, and values. There is no fellowship between the saved and the unsaved, nor with light and darkness.

Unfortunately, there have been many accounts of one proclaiming to be a believer to convince or impress others. They act like one and later prove not to be. This is where much prayer, fasting, and discernment are needed before agreeing to commit to the relationship. Take note of faith in action. It is easy for one to say he or she is a believer in our Lord Jesus, but is there evidence of:

- the fear of the Lord?
- the person having been born again of the Spirit of God?
- a commitment in serving the Lord through prayers, bible reading, and bible studies?
- fellowship and connection with the body of Christ?
- evidence of the Fruit of the Spirit?
- separation from worldly affairs and its ways?

Without this, there will be conflicts in the relationship because of the presence and conflict of light and darkness, which leads to being unequally yoked. There will be disagreements in different areas of our lives, as we are literally not walking together, but apart from each other as expressed in Amos 3:3 KJV, *"Can two walk together, except they be agreed?"*

1. Are there unresolved issues, especially relationship and family issues or traumas?

2. Is there a good family connection, especially with the male honoring his mother and the female having a good bond with her father? These are very important pointers. A male who does not honor his mother especially will most often not honor and care for his wife. I have observed this in many individuals and relationships. It is here the individuals learn to honor, respect, and care for their spouses.

3. Are there present or unresolved issues with substance abuse?

4. Is there any evidence of unhealthy social behaviors or relationships?

5. Are their previous relationships long or short-term? This demonstrates the ability to maintain a good relationship.

6. Does the individual have a good work ethic? This is a sign of stability or instability.

7. Is he/she able to resolve conflicts easily without resorting to blaming the other?

8. Do you share a lot in common, or are you opposite in many ways?

9. Are you able to communicate amicably?

10. Does he/she feel comfortable praying and reading God's Word and belonging to a church family?

11. Are there expressed desires for sexual intimacy before marriage?

This is an unhealthy approach, as according to God's Word, sexual intimacy should be reserved for marriage. A sexual relationship outside marriage creates a spiritual bond and knitting of the two individual souls as previously discussed and does not allow both individuals to bond in a healthy way. It is here the relationship is compromised, and unhealthy situations cannot be effectively dealt with as a spiritual marriage has already taken place.

This causes sin against their own bodies and sin against God and creates an open door for the enemy to disrupt the relationship. If no repentance, asking for God's forgiveness, this relationship can become the enemy's playground.

When this is avoided, the relationship is bonded by God Himself, and He is in the midst to perfect it in whatever way is needed. It is therefore very important to pray sincerely about our life partner and trust the Holy Spirit to lead us to the right person.

Not all marriages are ordained of God, and He has already made His perfect choice for us.

Most often there is safety in a relationship with the right soul mate, as God is in the midst of it. These are some of the benefits: True love, acceptance, appreciation, and understanding are present. You can pray together in any situation. Encouragement and building up of each other.

1. It strengthens your immune system, as regular sexual activity with your loving partner and peace of mind can benefit your immune system.

2. It increases financial security.

3. Unity and good decision-making are enhanced.

4. A blessed life ensues as God fulfills His promise of a commanded blessing according to Psalm 133.

5. The fruit of the womb, our children are blessed for many generations.

I pray by God's grace that if you are not yet married, you will seek the Lord for His soul mate for you. If you are already married, I also pray that you and your spouse will grow to be soulmates.

Pearl 11
Prepared To Propel

The call to be used by God does not come very easy, but because He knew us from before we were formed in our mother's womb and He knows our destiny and purpose, He called us and prepared us: *"Before I formed thee in the belly, I knew thee; and before thou camest forth out of the womb I sanctified thee, and I ordained thee a prophet unto the nations."* (Jeremiah 1:5 KJV).

God spoke those words to Jeremiah, and He speaks the same to all His children who are called by Him. He has a divine plan and a purpose for our lives as seen in Jeremiah 29:11 (KJV), *"For I know the thoughts that I think toward you says the Lord, thoughts of peace and not evil, to give you an expected end."*

Like the Good Shepherd He is, He protects us with His anointing from the enemy, and His anointing causes us to be joyful and victorious in everything, including our sufferings. It is the anointing that breaks the yoke, as referenced in Exodus 23:20-30 (KJV), "Behold, I send an Angel before you to keep you in the way and to bring you into the place which I have prepared. Beware of Him and obey His voice; do not provoke Him, for He will not pardon your transgressions; for My name is in Him."

As the Lord calls us, we will never be alone. He protects us and sends His angels to watch over us. He said He would not leave us comfortless but would send the Holy Spirit who would lead and guide us in all truth (John 14:18).

As we journey through life, we will face many obstacles — many tests and trials — but as we overcome, remember what we are called to do in 2 Corinthians:

"Blessed be the GOD, even Father of our LORD Jesus Christ, the Father of mercies and GOD of all comfort, who comforteth us in all our tribulation, that we may be able to comfort them which are in any troubles, so that we can comfort those in any trouble with the comfort we ourselves receive from God." (2 Corinthians 1:3-4 KJV)

We do not overcome our trials through reading a book but through the ministry and healing of the Holy Spirit. Remember, it is the anointing that breaks the yoke. We cannot succeed in the academic world without having attended school and the required training for our profession; likewise, we are called to minister and function in the Kingdom of God. We will be taught and raised up spiritually by the Holy Spirit:

"But the anointing which ye have received from Him abideth in you, and you do not need that anyone teach you; but as the same anointing

teacheth you all things, and is truth, and I not a lie, and as it hath taught you, ye shall abide in Him." (1 John 2:27 KJV)

We will encounter life's challenges, and with the help of the Holy Spirit, we will overcome them. We must surrender all our cares to Him and trust Him to see us through: "It shall come to pass in that day that his burden will be taken away from your shoulder, and his yoke from your neck, and the yoke will be destroyed because of the anointing oil." (Isaiah 10:27 KJV)

The Lord will most often bring people into our lives to stand with us. Many times, these are people who have faced similar challenges, and as they have overcome them, they come alongside us to help us. Likewise, as we have overcome, we should stand with those who need our help.

To minister effectively for the Lord, we must remember that it is for the glory of God, that His glorious name be exalted, not ours:

"But we have this treasure in earthen vessels, that the excellency of the power may be of God and not of us. We are troubled on every side, yet not distressed; we are perplexed, but not in despair. Persecuted, but not forsaken; cast down, but not destroyed; always bearing about in the body the dying of the Lord Jesus, that the life of Jesus also may be made manifest in our body. For we which live are always delivered unto death for Jesus' sake, that the life also of Jesus might be made manifest in our moral flesh." (2 Corinthians 4:7-11 KJV)

We see David who was called and prepared to slay the enemy of Israel, Goliath the Philistine giant, whom the people feared. Scripture tells us that the people were "dismayed and greatly afraid" (1 Samuel 17:11 KJV), *"When Saul and all Israel heard those words of the Philistines, they were dismayed, and greatly afraid."*

David received his training as he took care of the sheep in the desert filled with wild animals. He fought them and killed them as he spared the lives of the sheep he tenderly cared for. Likewise, we too should use the strategies and the weapons given to us by the Holy Spirit and the Word of God. Remember the Lord's word to me in the call — "If you have not experienced this, you cannot reach out to those in that situation."

David was confident that the Lord was with him. He did not need the armor they were equipping him with. He was already equipped with God's power as seen in 1 Samuel 17:37 (KJV): *"Moreover,"* David said, *"The Lord that delivered me out of the paw of the lion, and out of the paw of the bear, He will deliver me out of the hand of this Philistine. And Saul said unto David, go, and the LORD be with thee."*

Who or what has God delivered you from? In what area or areas of life have you been tested, tried, and delivered? It was for a purpose; it was not to destroy you, take away your hope, or rob you of a future. It was for God's purpose; that was your training ground. By God's grace, let us respond to the call and be His hands extended in this hurting world. Let's position ourselves to bring hope to those who are in despair and pain. A scripture the Lord gave me in this calling was from Isaiah 61.

Prayer

Heavenly Father, I thank You for saving me through Your death on the cross. I also thank You for Your faithfulness to never leave nor forsake me but to be with me to the very end. You were always with me in every trial, which by Your grace made me stronger.

I answer Your call to follow You and to serve You...to be Your disciple. I thank You for preparing me so that I will be equipped to minister to Your hurting children. By Your grace, Father, I will, through the help of the Holy Spirit. Please help me to be faithful to Your call. I give myself to You so You can use me.

Thank You, Father.
It's in the precious, matchless, and powerful name of Jesus I pray.
Amen

Pearl 12
My Personal Deliverances

During a transformative weekend retreat with Women's Aglow, I had a profound encounter that led to my deliverance. As my roommates and I settled into our room, I found myself under a sudden attack from the enemy. A demonic spirit manifested itself before me, entering our room. At the time, I was a young believer filled with the Spirit, but I lacked the experience and knowledge to effectively respond to such a situation. The manifestation occurred while my two roommates and I gathered to pray before supper and our first evening session.

As we engaged in prayer, uttering prayers in tongues, an unsettling change came over my voice, indicating that the demonic spirit had taken hold of me. The experience was undeniably frightening, as I realized I was being possessed by this malevolent entity. It became apparent that the demon was aware of the freedom and deliverance that awaited me during that very weekend.

I am immensely grateful to the Lord for blessing me with such wonderful and spiritually mature roommates. One of them held the esteemed position of President in a local Women's Aglow chapter. We had previously developed a deep friendship, and she graciously extended an invitation for me to be one of her roommates for the retreat.

It is indeed beneficial to connect ourselves with mature women in the Lord, as they can serve as mentors and catalysts for our growth. I strongly sensed that the orchestration of rooming with my spiritually mature roommates for that weekend was guided by the Holy Spirit Himself. It became evident that this arrangement was part of a divine plan.

Both of my roommates immediately recognized the spiritual warfare at hand and swiftly entered a mode of intense prayer. It served as a powerful reminder that the enemy is always vigilant, seeking opportunities to steal, kill, and destroy, as stated in John 10:10 (KJV) *"The thief cometh not, but for to steal, and to kill, and to destroy. I am come that they might have life, and that they might have it more abundantly."*

The very first night of the retreat, a significant dream unfolded before me. In this dream, I found myself in the presence of the Lord, alongside my ex-husband, within the serene beauty of a heavenly open park. A question emerged within me, filled with curiosity and a tinge of disbelief: How did he, after all the cruelty he had shown me, find his place here? Could it be that he had finally surrendered his life to the Lord? The weight of anticipation hung in the air as I sensed the Lord examining us, preparing to reveal our "scores" for the end-of-time judgment. Inwardly, I wondered what his score would be, assuming that his acts of evil would surely diminish his standing. To my astonishment, he scored ninety-eight out of one hundred. A wave of amazement washed over me as I concluded *He must have repented and surrendered to the Lord.*

Then came my turn to be scored. As the Lord placed a miniature version of myself on a table, a single effortless motion of His hand revealed an unsettling truth — a wound, an unhealed wound, nestled deep within the core of my chest. Instantly, I recognized the lingering pain that resided within me. With gentle yet powerful fingers, the Lord parted the wound, exposing its depth.

Dear saints, this is the consequence of our woundedness — a real and profound incision that, if left untreated, remains open, vulnerable to the infiltration of spiritual infections. These infections manifest as hatred, anger, resentment, an inability to trust, and an overwhelming sense of unworthiness, among others. Their repercussions are far-reaching:

- Mental and emotional disorders
- Psychological struggles
- Physical afflictions, including cardiac diseases, ulcerative colitis, Crohn's disease, and various cancers
- Autoimmune disorders

As the Lord continued to delve into my heart, He laid bare the unhealed wound and the insidious infestations it harbored. I was deeply wounded, plagued by spiritual infections. Unless we experience healing and deliverance, these infections permeate our being, resulting in a host of illnesses that overrun our spiritual selves. Drawing from my background as a nurse, the Lord graciously revealed to me the intricate process and outcomes of bleeding, mirroring the state of my own wounded heart. Below I will uncover the three layers that are formed as a consequence of our brokenness as was seen in my dream.

1. The first layer that I encountered was **frozen blood** — a state in which the Lord revealed to me as the effects of various forms of hurt, whether physical, verbal, emotional, mental, or spiritual. When we experience these wounds, bleeding occurs within our spirits. It is during this time that we often become cold, withdrawn, and isolated.

2. Beneath the frozen blood, I witnessed the presence of **clotted blood**. Over time, the fresh and frozen blood transforms into clots — a natural response of the body to stop the bleeding. However, if clotting does not occur naturally, the bleeding persists.

3. Unveiling the third layer, I beheld a disturbing sight — a **putrefied and gangrenous substance**. The Lord revealed to me that within this layer, malignancy takes hold, with the most common manifestation being cancer.

Continuing with my dream, I witnessed the Lord scooping out these layers of turmoil and decay from within me. I am forever grateful for the beautiful hand of our Lord, gently removing the three layers of debris that had plagued my heart. Throughout the cleansing process, He spoke to me, reminding me that despite my deep wounds, I had been a blessing to others.

After the Lord healed me, He understood the importance of a tangible symbol to represent His love and restoration in my life, something I could bring back to my family. With skilled craftsmanship, He fashioned a circular wreath using a special material commonly used for ribbons and other artistic creations. I marveled at how effortlessly He unraveled the ribbon, and I noticed that its color perfectly matched the hues of my family room. Intrigued, I couldn't help but ask the Lord how He knew the color of my family room. In that moment, I reminded myself and admitted to Him that I had forgotten He knows everything.

Spiritually, I gained a clear understanding of the significance behind this round wreath. It symbolized a love that is unbroken, much like a wedding ring represents the bond between two souls. The color, reflecting the essence of my family, indicated that the Lord had crafted this circle of love specifically for me to carry back to them.

As I awakened from my dream, an incredible sense of freedom and excitement filled my spirit, knowing that the Lord had cleansed and delivered me. The weight of all the inner turmoil and mess was gone, and I never felt so light and liberated.

The following night, however, I experienced another dream that stirred up fear and anxiety, bringing back memories of physical attacks from my ex-husband. In the dream, he wielded a machete and struck me three times — a haunting reflection of the three occasions when I had to call the police due to his violent behavior in the past. When I finally woke up, the dream felt eerily real, and fear gripped my heart. I felt an urgent need for someone to pray for me. However, my friend was not present in the room, and my other roommate was sound asleep. Reluctant to disturb her, I sensed a strong conviction that the Lord wanted my undivided attention without involving anyone else. The Holy Spirit spoke to my heart, saying, "Get up and come with me. I want you to pray about this on your own." It was clear that He desired a one-on-one encounter.

Without hesitation, I rose from my bed and found a quiet spot in a small sitting area outside our room. Uncertain of what to expect or what actions to take, I trusted that the Holy Spirit would guide me. Deep within, I knew I was not alone.

As I sat down, I poured out my heart to the Holy Spirit, confessing my lack of knowledge on how to proceed. I asked for His help, and in an instant, it was as though I was watching a television screen before me. I saw the word "FORGIVE" rolling across the screen. Surprised, I responded, "Lord, I thought I had already forgiven him." The Holy Spirit gently revealed, "You may have spoken the words, but true forgiveness did not come from your heart." Recognizing my need for assistance, I implored Him to help me, and instantaneously, with sincerity, I released the burden of unforgiveness towards my exhusband.

Immediately after forgiving my ex-husband from the depths of my soul with the help of the Holy Spirit, I experienced a profound outpouring of the Lord's sweet love flowing into me. It was a love so incredibly sweet and intoxicating that, in the natural, I struggled to fully comprehend or bear its intensity. It overwhelmed me to the point where it felt like I was gasping for breath as if I couldn't take it all in. I had to request the Lord to pause, as His love was just too overwhelming for me to handle. It was a reminder of the truth expressed in scripture that God's love is sweet, much sweeter than the honeycomb: "More to be desired are they than gold, yea, than much fine gold: sweeter also than honey and the honeycomb." (Psalm 19:10 KJV)

I once had the pleasure of having some honey from the honeycomb, and I can honestly tell you, it is sweet and very intoxicating. It can leave you drunk, and only a small portion can be eaten.

God's love, which was so richly poured into me, began to pour out of me and to those close to me who were affected by the unforgiveness within me.

At that moment, I instantly had an open vision where I saw my ex as though he was standing on a street before me, and love for him began to flow from my heart. I also began to experience such intense love for my now husband and children, especially my son Chris who so much reminded me of his biological father. I was instantly healed and delivered of unforgiveness, and God's rich and bountiful love filled that void. I couldn't wait to return to share with my family and ask them to forgive me and just love on them. I felt totally set free and couldn't wait to make the exact wreath the Lord made and hang it in our family room as a reminder of His deliverance and love for my family. The journey of healing and restoration continues as we navigate through the adversities and pains of life. It is an ongoing process that accompanies us until we depart from this earth.

During one particular night after experiencing the initial healing, I found myself curled up in a corner of my bedroom, clutching my chest in intense agony. In the midst of a dream, I felt excruciating pain surging through my chest. In the dream, I witnessed as the Lord gently but decisively tore away the outer muscular layer of my heart, the myocardium. I saw my heart held in His hand, blood dripping freely. Remarkably, there was no anesthesia administered before this procedure. The Lord later conveyed to me that He purposely withheld the anesthesia to allow me to feel the depth of pain I would have endured had He not intervened. It was a vivid portrayal of the profound suffering we experience when we are wounded deep within our souls, wreaking havoc in our lives and causing significant harm.

This powerful imagery highlighted the importance of acknowledging and addressing the depth of our emotional and spiritual wounds. It emphasized the significance of allowing ourselves to truly experience the pain, so that true healing and restoration can take place.

In that moment, I understood that the Lord was not only healing the external manifestations of my pain, but also addressing the core of my being, the innermost chambers of my heart. His intention was to bring about a complete and thorough healing that would permeate every aspect of my being, leaving no residue of brokenness behind.

While the experience was intense and unsettling, it served as a poignant reminder of the depth of God's love and His commitment to our restoration. He was willing to walk alongside me, even in the midst of pain, to bring about healing that was profound, lasting, and transformative.

Also, as we mentioned, I encourage you to seek professional and spiritual help when you are experiencing situations that cause emotional pain and disruption to your peace. Get someone to pray for you if you are not able to pray for yourself. Do not live with this type of pain. Not only does it affect you, but it also affects those dearest to you. God is gracious and merciful. He will never abandon us; He is always available to save, heal, and deliver us.

I also encourage you to spend time in God's Word, in prayer, and completely trust the Holy Spirit, who will reveal areas in our lives where healing and deliverance are needed to make us whole. Remember, The Lord sees and knows our deepest thoughts and pains.

Nothing is hidden from Him, not even our deepest thoughts or whispers. He is always available and desires to set us free. This is the time He is even closer to us: *"The LORD is nigh unto them that are of a broken heart; and saveth such as be of a contrite spirit."* (Psalm 34:18 KJV).

Take time to read and meditate on Isaiah 61. God's favor is upon us because He desires to set us free. He came to:

- Bind up the brokenhearted
- Proclaim freedom for the captives
- And release prisoners from darkness

This entire scripture deals with every area of our woundedness and imprisonment. Let us choose to be free in the Lord and be set free.

<u>Self-Reflection</u>

What is your current emotional status on a scale of 1-10 (with 10 being the highest)?

1. Can you identify any area of discomfort in your life where healing is needed?

   _____

2. Are you experiencing hatred or resentment towards anyone?

   _____

3. Is there someone in your life you need to forgive for having caused you pain?

   _____

4. Are you feeling angry, sad, fearful, anxious, or in pain?

   _____

5. Are you experiencing any physical ailments that you can possibly relate to your emotional status?

   _____

6. Are you experiencing trust issues?

   _____

7. Are you experiencing difficulties in releasing and forgiving?

   _____

8. If you are feeling any of the above, what is your plan of action to change your situation?_

   _____

Prayer

Heavenly Father,

I pray for this precious soul who is experiencing a lot of emotional pain deep within the recesses of their soul. I ask You to deliver them of all their pain and suffering, their loneliness, and sadness within. Please help this reader to forgive and release his/her pain and to forgive those who caused them pain.

Deliver those who have been emotionally, mentally, spiritually, and physically abused. Whatever is causing them stress, grief, and sorrow, I ask You to heal them and set them free from any bondage.

For those, dear Lord, who are experiencing the pain of a broken relationship, marriage difficulties, separation, divorce, rejection, or betrayal, I ask You Lord to please heal and deliver them. Help them to forgive those who have caused them such pain.

I ask that you bless them with Your peace which passes all human understanding. Let them sense and experience Your love, which never fails. Please pour Your healing balm upon their painful wounds and set them free from their pain and imprisonment.

In Your precious and mighty name, I pray.

Amen

Pearl 13
God's Precious Pearls Ministry

"And they shall be Mine, saith the LORD of Hosts, in that day when I make up My jewels; and I will spare them, as a man spareth his own son that serveth him." (Malachi 3:17 KJV)

The Birthing of God's Precious Pearls Ministry

Before we can be of help to others, we must experience healing as described in my "personal deliverances." As we experience healing, we help to bring comfort to those in similar situations:

"Blessed be the God, even the Father of our Lord Jesus Christ, the Father of mercies, and the God of all comfort; who comforteth us in all our tribulation, that we be able to comfort them which are in any trouble, with the comfort where with we ourselves are comforted of God." (2 Corinthians 1:3-4 KJV)

As I devoted my time to studying God's Word, He confirmed His call on my life through Isaiah 61. It was during worship that the Lord spoke to my heart. He said:

My daughter, some women cannot give nor receive because their foundation is broken. Tell them their only way to receive is to be healed from their broken and shattered foundation and apply the Fruits of My Spirit to their lives. The Fruits of the Spirit are the essence and entity of My character. It is only through Me they can be healed and live a fruitful and productive life.

He led me to His Word in Isaiah 61 and the Fruits of the Spirit in Galatians 5:16-26. These scriptures became the foundation of the call on my life, God's Precious Pearls.

God's Precious Pearls is a ministry of healing and deliverance for God's daughters, those whose hearts have been wounded and shattered through various adversities in life. Whatever brought us pain, God is able to heal, restore, and set us free to become His beautiful and beloved bride.

We are God's Precious Pearls. We became His precious gems, by having received Him as our Lord and Savior, our healer, our redeemer, and our restorer. We face adversities daily, but as long as we are anchored in Him, we are safe:

"We are troubled in every side, yet not distressed; we are perplexed, but not in despair; persecuted, but not forsaken; cast down, but not destroyed; always bearing about in the body the dying of the LORD Jesus, that the life also of Jesus might be made manifest in our body. For we which live are always delivered unto death for Jesus' sake, that the life also of Jesus might be made manifest in our mortal flesh. So that death worketh in us." (2 Corinthians 4:8-12 KJV)

A Pearl is formed within the shell of the oyster through irritation from a parasite or a grain of sand. The oyster secretes a substance called nacre, which covers the sand or parasite. Layer by layer, this is covered, and from this, a pearl is formed. Likewise, as we face various adversities, the Holy Spirit covers us and protects us as we yield to Him and abide in His secret place. A continuous release and ministry of His anointing protects us, builds us up, heals us, and then delivers us. Through this process, we are cultured into the beautiful Pearl and the image of our Lord Jesus Christ, bearing the marks of His suffering.

Just as the nacre covers the irritating substance and the pearl is formed, so does the Lord cover and shield us during trials and adversities with the oil of His anointing and the ministry of the Holy Spirit:

"He that dwelleth in the secret place of the Most High shall abide under the shadow of the Almighty. I will say of the LORD, He is my refuge and my fortress: my God: in Him will I trust. Surely, He shall deliver thee from the snare of the fowler, and from the noisome pestilence. He shall cover thee with His feathers, and under His wings shalt thou trust: His truth shall be thy shield and buckler." (Psalm 91:1-3 KJV)

Our becoming like Jesus does not happen overnight; this is an ongoing process while we are cultured and formed into His image as the precious Holy Spirit teaches us the Word of God, which cleanses, heals, convicts, and changes us. We are then conformed to the image of our

Lord Jesus Christ. We are changed from glory to glory: "But we all, with open face beholding as in a glass the glory of the Lord, are changed into the same image from glory to glory, even as by the Spirit of the Lord" (2 Corinthians 3:18 KJV).

God's Precious Pearls Ministry was birthed out of the pain and brokenness of my first marriage. I honestly did not realize how broken and fragmented I was until the Lord took hold of me and brought me to a place of healing and deliverance. This was an ongoing process over a few years as the Holy Spirit taught and mentored me through His Word, worship, and prayer.

There are different qualities of pearls, so with more pain and more yielding to the ministry of the Holy Spirit, we are made into that exceptional, rare, and beautiful pearl, one that is flawless with a sparkle. The exceptionally good and expensive pearl is cultured naturally, especially those that come from the very depths of the ocean. When we experience deep pain, as we are surrendered to the Lord, we come out as gold: "But He knoweth the way that I take: when He hath tried me, I shall come forth as gold" (Job 23:10 KJV).

After the birth of my fourth child Jon, my quest to learn the deeper things of God increased. I was drawn by the Holy Spirit for a deeper walk with Him. I began to cry out for more of God as I discerned there was more than what I was taught. I developed an unquenchable thirst for God because there was more outside the confines of my denominational church. I remember sweeping the floor of my foyer one morning when I tossed the broom and began to cry out to God, "Oh God, there is more of You! I need all of You! Dear God, help me! I need to learn more about You! There is more about You that I have not been taught!" This was indeed the drawing of the Holy Spirit on my heart. This was an extraordinarily strong tug in my spirit, so strong that I tossed the broom and went into prayer and yielded to the Holy Spirit.

God loves us, and He has a plan and purpose for each of us. It is His precious Holy Spirit Who draws us to Him. Have you ever felt that tug in your spirit? Do not ignore it; surrender, and yield to the Holy Spirit's calling: "No man can come to Me, except the Father which hath sent me draw him; and I will raise him up at the last day" (John 6:44 KJV). Do not question the visitation and ministry of the Holy Spirit, and do not wait for someone to lay hands on you. Submit to the yielding and ministry of the Holy Spirit and the Word of God.

The Lord heard and answered my prayers. I was invited to the Women's Aglow International Women's Fellowship by one of my coworkers. I could not wait to get there, and I did not want to be late. The ladies were busily preparing the place of fellowship when I arrived with my infant son Jon, who was only four weeks old. I found a quiet corner to nurse him, as I was early for the meeting.

It was after the time of fellowship and ministry that I joined the prayer line where the speaker prayed for me. She said, "Honey, did you hear what The Lord said about you?

Is your name Pearlene? You are 'God's precious pearl.' You are locked away in a shell at the bottom of the ocean. The Lord said He is going to clean you up, culture you, and polish you, and when He is finished, He is going to let you out of that shell for the world to see."

Those words resonated deeply within my soul and were powerful seeds sown into my spirit, which began to grow as I yielded to the ministry of the Holy Spirit and was watered in God's Word, with much prayer and waiting on Him. I had not told this minister my name; the Holy Spirit, in His divine wisdom, revealed my identity to the minister, confirming the Lord's involvement and guidance in my healing journey.

As this precious anointed woman of God, the late Rev. Ruth Heflin, ministered to me, I visualized the polishing process. I knew the following points:

1. It would be painful, but I was ready to stand the pain. I assured myself that I would not be afraid because I was ready to submit to the hands of the Master Potter. I reassured myself that the Lord would help me to withstand the pain and He would teach me. I did not know about the work and power of the Holy Spirit because I was yet not baptized in His power.

2. It would not just happen overnight or in days, weeks, or months. I did not anticipate years, but praise the Lord, God's timing is altogether perfect. The process will continue until we see our sweet Jesus face to face.

I felt that my journey in the "School of the Holy Spirit," had begun. I felt such love and tenderness as I was methodically taught by Him. Scripture tells us that the Holy Spirit will teach us things that we do not know. Great mysteries and revelations from God's Word began to unfold through the teaching of the Holy Spirit.

I was very eager to learn, so I sat under the teaching and ministry of the Holy Spirit through these older, loving, and caring women. Every Tuesday, I attended bible study in one of the leader's homes. We considered her lovely living room our "nursery" where we younger women grew in the Lord. We were prayed for and experienced deliverances many times.

I later became an official member of Women's Aglow and the worship leader for our local chapter. It was not long after that I received the baptism of the Holy Spirit with the evidence of speaking in tongues. (See Acts 2:4 about the baptism of the Holy Spirit.)

I knew and recognized the periods of polishing, which were sometimes very lonely and painful. In the privacy of my prayer closet, I found solace in pouring out my heart to God, shedding tears and making a commitment to wait on Him and trust Him completely. Surrendering my heart to Him, I became fully submitted to His will.

This transformative process is ongoing as long as I reside in this earthly vessel, continuously bringing glory to God until my departure from this world.

Do not hesitate to pour out your tears before the Lord, for He ministers to you in the depths of your soul through the Holy Spirit's loving touch. He reaches into those wounded areas, bathing them with His love, washing and purifying them profoundly.

Throughout this journey, I experienced numerous moments of healing and personal deliverance as I spent intimate time alone with the Lord. He graciously addressed the deep-seated hurts that had manifested in various ways, such as anger, low self-esteem, and a pervasive sense of identity loss. I entered my present marriage carrying burdensome baggage that had been hidden from my awareness. Sometimes, we mistakenly believe we are healed when we are not. Yet, I remained patient, knowing that God was perfecting His will for me: "But let patience have her perfect work, that ye may be perfect and entire, wanting nothing" (James 1:4 KJV).

The priceless transformation into the image of our Savior requires time and great patience. It is during these precious moments that true healing occurs, and the fruit of the Spirit is nurtured in our lives as we devote ourselves to Him. The sweet aroma of our Savior's presence becomes evident, uniting us in a common bond of peace (Ephesians 4:3).

It was one morning during my quiet time with the Lord, I saw a beautiful iridescent pearl waiting to be released, but there were weeds on the shell, so the Holy Spirit had to work more with me. There were other areas in my life where much healing was needed. In my spirit, I heard, *I am ready to come out, but not on that dirty shell.* The Holy Spirit had to do His work within me; now it was my time to surrender and release all imperfect areas in my life. I needed to be healed, not only within, but outwardly as well. The Lord makes us beautiful inside and out. It is by our fruits that we are known. What fruit or fruits did I have to work on? I had to search my heart and surrender all bad fruits to Him.

It was about that time when I had the dream of the Lord ripping the outer layer of my heart. He had to remove the callous layer of my heart in order to make it pliable and tender so that I would not have a heart of stone but a heart of flesh.

The Launching of God's Precious Pearls Ministry

I saw the release of the beautiful pearl from the shell. The shell glowed with such luster. The Holy Spirit spoke to my heart: "Go forth my daughter as My precious pearl. Bring healing and restoration to my daughters; I will bring them to you." God's Precious Pearls Ministry was birthed in 1993 when the Lord began to use me to write encouraging monthly letters throughout the United States, United Kingdom, and Jamaica. Those newsletters ministered to those who were hurting and needed healing and encouragement with an "on time" word from the Lord. He again reminded me of the scripture from 2 Corinthians 1:3-5. This scripture is repeated many times in this book, and it is indeed the foundation of our ministry through our journey with the Lord.

He then began to lead His hurting daughters to me with various problems, mainly relational and marital problems. Many traveled for miles as we met in my home on a set day each week for worship, prayer, healing, and deliverance. Many were delivered and set free under the power of the Holy Spirit. I was also blessed with the opportunity to minister on many occasions in the church where I was raised in my hometown in Jamaica. The work of God's Precious Pearls Ministry continues today.

We cannot impart what we do not have and have not been delivered from, so it is with our testimony that we are able, with the help of the Holy Spirit, to minister with love and compassion to those who are hurting. Remember Jesus was familiar with our sufferings according to Isaiah 53. Scripture tells us that Jesus was moved with compassion as He ministered: *"But when He saw the multitudes, He was moved with compassion for them, because they fainted, and scattered abroad, as sheep having no shepherd."* (Matthew 9:36-38 KJV).

We cannot minister His healing by reading books. Through our own personal pain and suffering, we become familiar with others who are suffering, and through the equipping of the Holy Spirit, we become our Lord's hands extended, thus releasing His healing power and setting the captives free.

Holy Spirit then led me to Isaiah 61 and described to me the work He had prepared me for. A deep passion for those who were hurting was birthed within me. I began to see the pain in their faces, and even pain that was camouflaged through faint smiles became obvious as revealed through the Holy Spirit. Immediately after that, the Lord began to bring women into my path. I met them in different crossroads in life; some in the grocery store, others at church, and many at the hospital where I worked. These women were hurting in many ways. I ministered to them at their locations as the Holy Spirit led me.

For that reason, I chose to work in mental health as a registered nurse, where I saw various types and degrees of pain and addictions and ministered through the open door of availability. There was more freedom for ministry when I worked within a Christian-oriented treatment facility. This was also a spiritual training ground for me as the Holy Spirit taught and led me.

While ministering in my home, there was a sister who had endured a traumatic experience in her past, which she briefly mentioned during our conversation. However, the Holy Spirit whispered to me, "It is not over. The pain lingers." Moved by His promptings, I courageously relayed His message to her. Suddenly, without any physical contact, she fell to the floor while still seated. Rolling from one end of the room to the other, the Holy Spirit unraveled all the hidden pain that had been festering within her. When she finally rose from the floor, it was evident that she had been completely transformed. This sister had been accustomed to wearing dark and oversized garments, using them as a means to conceal her pain and shame. However, the morning before our subsequent meeting, the Holy Spirit spoke to my heart once again. I was to convey to her that she would no longer need to wear dark and large clothing. Knowing her joy in creating her own garments, I eagerly shared this divine message with her when she arrived at my home for ministry. To her astonishment, she revealed that the Holy Spirit had communicated the exact same thing to her that very morning as she was gathering fabric to make a new outfit.

As the days unfolded, we witnessed a remarkable change in her countenance. Her eyes, no longer clouded with darkness, now sparkled with brightness. She exuded a newfound joy, laughter, and freedom. The radiant transformation brought forth the beautiful radiance of the Lord that enveloped her entire being.

On that same morning, a new sister joined our gathering, having witnessed the remarkable transformation and radiance in the sister who had previously been ministered to. Moved by what she saw, she expressed her own desire to experience the same encounter. As we gathered in prayer, the Holy Spirit once again manifested His power, gently causing her to fall to the floor in submission to His ministry. There, He personally ministered to her, releasing her from the chains of her past and bringing forth complete deliverance. She also arose with the glory of God on her face.

Since then, God's Precious Pearls Ministry has continued to flourish with a devoted group of sisters who share a deep love for the Lord. Together, we devote ourselves to the study of God's Word, engage in heartfelt worship, and fervently pray, with weekly conference call Prayer meetings twice a week. In our midst, we encounter ongoing deliverance, healing, and restoration. Our spiritual growth is nurtured as we immerse ourselves in His wisdom and grace, and we find ourselves transformed day by day.

The journey of God's Precious Pearls Ministry is a testament to His unfailing love and the power of unity among believers. As we walk together, we embrace the divine purpose of being transformed into the image of Christ, eagerly anticipating the ongoing work of the Holy Spirit in our lives.

My Purpose for God's Precious Pearl

■ To witness God's daughters set free from their pain and suffering, experiencing complete wholeness as they step into the fullness of who He has ordained them to be: "For I know the thoughts that I think toward you, says the LORD, thoughts of peace and not of evil, to give you an expected end" (Jeremiah 29:11 KJV). It is crucial to identify the source of our pain and trust the Lord to bring healing and freedom, enabling us to shine as the beautiful "Pearls" we were created to be for His glory.

■ To help women grasp their true identity in Christ Jesus. We are immensely special to Him, and He laid down His life to set us free. Through His sacrificial love, He bore our sins and shame on the cross, redeeming us from the enemy's lies and enslavement. We are now precious gems in the eyes of our Heavenly Father, His royal bride, and beloved princesses. When we fully grasp our identity in Him, we are empowered to embrace our calling and occupy the places He has prepared for us.

■ Following the instruction of Titus 2:3-5, we aim to teach and guide younger women to live holy lives before God. I encourage them to be sober-minded, to love their husbands and children, to be discreet, chaste, keepers of their homes, and obedient to their own husbands. By following these principles, we ensure that the word of God is not blasphemed, and we foster a culture of godliness and righteousness.

■ Here at God's Precious Pearls Ministry, we are committed to supporting those facing various difficulties in their singleness and marriage. Our desire is to teach, assist, and minister to them as the Lord leads. I pray that this prepares you to connect with the right purpose partner God has in store for you. For those who are already married, I recognize that God's design for the home and marriage is sacred and should be exalted for His glory. The enemy despises our homes and seeks to destroy our marriages, so it is vital to equip ourselves with knowledge of his tactics and to overcome them through the power of God's Word and His Spirit.

By pursuing these purposes, God's Precious Pearls Ministry seeks to impact the lives of women, empowering them to walk in the freedom, purpose, and fulfillment that God has destined for them. It is essential to acknowledge that functioning adequately becomes challenging when we carry deep wounds and unresolved brokenness from our past hurts and trauma. As the saying goes, "Hurt people hurt people." It becomes impossible to pour into the lives of others when our own cup is empty and depleted. In order to effectively serve and help others, we must first receive healing and deliverance from our own pain.

Transformation occurs when we allow God to turn our wounds into beauty marks, and when His healing touch transforms our scars into precious reminders of His restoration. Through the deep healing that only God can provide, we are able to find wholeness and emerge as vessels of His love and grace.

By addressing our own wounds and allowing God to bring healing and deliverance, we are better equipped to extend genuine compassion, empathy, and support to those around us. It is from a place of healed brokenness that we can effectively minister to others, offering them hope and pointing them toward the same transformative healing that we have experienced.

Recognizing the importance of personal healing, we emphasize the journey of allowing God to heal and transform us for His glory by embracing this process, we are able to serve others from a place of strength, compassion, and authenticity, shining the light of God's healing and restoration into their lives.

God's Precious Pearls Ministry is available to minister wherever needed so that the children of God will be set free and be delivered through the power of the Holy Spirit from all that hinders them in life's journey so that they may fulfill their destiny and glorify God.

Personal Reflection

The significance of providing abundant help and guidance towards healing is crucial, particularly in situations like mine. In today's world, where the global pandemic of COVID-19 has led to an increase in mental health problems, divorce, and various forms of abuse, the need for addressing these issues is more urgent than ever. Women, in particular, have experienced heightened levels of abuse during this pandemic, including mental, physical, and emotional mistreatment. Tragically, there have been reports of sexual abuse involving children, as well as a surge in marital breakdowns and divorces.

Throughout the entire land, the hearts of precious little souls are torn as moms and dads are no longer together, and some children spend their early growing years in separate homes. This unfortunately has become the norm too many.

Moved by compassion and a deep sense of obedience, I have answered the call to author this book. Through sharing my testimony, I believe that you, too, can experience God's mighty healing power and find deliverance and freedom from all the pain, imprisonment, and bondages you may be facing. My prayer is that through reading these words, you, my dear readers, will come to know the mighty, caring, and loving God we serve. Our Heavenly Father is deeply concerned about every aspect of our lives, and He promises to perfect all that concerns us and bring healing to our broken and troubled souls.

When we experience the shattering of a relationship in any form, whether it's a friendship, engagement, or divorce, it's important to understand that the Lord is with us every step of the way. In the case of a profound connection where our souls are intertwined with another person, causing us to become one flesh, the pain we endure goes beyond mere betrayal and broken trust. There is a deep tearing within the recesses of our souls, resulting in immense pain and woundedness. This internal turmoil can lead to physical ailments and diseases, some of which can be devastating. Moreover, if left unhealed and unaddressed, the effects can permeate future generations, impacting our children. Let us love our children enough to seek deliverance for ourselves so that they may not have to experience what we have endured.

I express my gratitude to my parents, family members, and friends for their prayers and unwavering support, which has blessed and carried me through those difficult times. There were moments when I felt isolated and alone, and their encouragement and prayers played a vital role in my healing process. This experience has also made me more attentive to those around me who are going through similar situations, offering them encouragement and healing. Through this challenging journey, I have grown closer to the Lord, experiencing His love and faithfulness in countless ways. I have been forever transformed by these trying circumstances.

If you, like me, have been a victim and an overcomer, let us make ourselves available to help others in need of healing and restoration as we are led. It is an honor and a humbling experience to be called by God to minister His love, healing, and deliverance to His precious children. Recognizing our own unworthiness, we become extensions of the Lord's hands, submissive to the leading of the Holy Spirit. Trusting in His guidance, discernment, direction, and anointing, we rely on the Holy Spirit's power. As stated in Zechariah 4:6 (KJV), *"... not by might, nor by power, but by my Spirit, says the LORD of hosts."*

As I reflect on my life's journey, I am reminded of how the Lord has led and personally taught me through various tests and trials, including this difficult path. The Holy Spirit has been my primary source of training, providing experiential wisdom from God. Consistent worship, prayer, and immersion in His Word have strengthened and prepared me for the ministry I now undertake.

It is crucial to recognize that we pose a threat to the enemy's plans. His intent is to discourage, accuse, and derail us, robbing us of God's blessings. The enemy will stop at nothing to prevent God's children from finding freedom, placing obstacles and troubles in our paths. Is it comfortable? Absolutely not! Experiencing pain, rejection, and resentment from those we love and care for deeply is excruciating. There were moments of profound sorrow and private anguish when I poured out my heart to the Lord, who comforted me.

This, too, wounds the soul when we expose our hearts, only to have them torn apart by those we love and care for. However, I have learned not to fear because nothing is hidden from the Lord. He fights our battles on our behalf, and I have experienced the power of casting my cares upon Him because He genuinely cares for me. As He reminds us in Matthew 11:28-30 (KJV), "Come unto me, all ye that labor and are heavy laden, and I will give you rest. Take my yoke upon you and learn from me, for I am meek and lowly in heart, and you shall find rest unto your souls. For my yoke is easy, and my burden is light." There is absolutely nothing that remains hidden from Him.

This painful journey has deepened my love and trust in Him. I have witnessed His mighty hand moving in my life, having delivered me from a painful marriage and brought me to my now husband for His purpose and glory. I want to encourage you, my readers, that the Lord will do the same and even more for you.

My answer and healing came through forgiveness, fervent prayer for my ex-husband, and surrendering to the leading and ministry of the Holy Spirit and His Word. I am confident in the continued watchful care of the Holy Spirit, who shields and hides me. It is my responsibility to remain steadfast and grounded in Him, guarding my heart with diligence, and trusting in His wisdom, discernment, and guidance.

Just as a marriage relationship is an intimate reflection of God's love for His bride, so is our relationship as children after God's own heart. We cannot embark on a calling to touch the lives of God's precious children without intimately knowing Him. We must experience His love and mighty power, which enables us to move in His authority.

I am assured of the peace of the Lord as I pursue intimacy with Him, fully aware that *"in Him we live and move and have our being."* (Acts 17:28 NIV). There is no need to fear because His perfect love casts out all fear. I have resolved to *"take up my cross daily and follow Him."* (Luke 9:23) KJV as well as *"dying to self daily"* (1 Corinthians 15:31 KJV) as I have learned through this arduous journey.

In these dark and trying days, let us be sensitive to those around us who are hurting in so many ways, and in need of our prayers, comforting words, and healing touch. Time is of the essence, and the signs of our Lord's return is evident all around us. I am fearful of not completing the task the Lord has called me to do. Therefore, with the help of the Holy Spirit, I have answered the call to share His love and healing through this book.

As you read, I pray that the Holy Spirit ministers to you exactly where you need it most. May you be completely healed, delivered, and set free from all that has robbed you of joy and peace in the Lord. I pray for healing in the deepest recesses of your soul, that your broken heart may be mended and healed, making you whole. If you have been held captive spiritually, may you experience liberation as the prison doors open wide in Jesus' mighty name.

May you find consolation and comfort as you release all your cares, burdens, and sorrows to the Lord, who has been eagerly waiting for you to come to Him with all your pain. Instead of sorrow, travail, and ashes, everything around you will become beautiful as God, who sees and knows your pain, vindicates you and sets you free. In place of garments of heaviness, you will be adorned with garments of praise unto the Lord.

I pray that as you submit to Him, mourning will be replaced with joy, praise, and dancing before the Lord, and all your sorrows will flee from you. May the Lord bless you, keep you, deliver you, and use you for His glory.

Remember, *"you are a tree of righteousness, planted by the Lord,"* (Isaiah 61:3 KJV) that He may be glorified through you. You were created in His image; He loves you, and by His stripes, you are healed. May healing be yours today, and may you be set free in Jesus' mighty name. Amen.

Prayer

Heavenly Father,

I thank You for Your love for me. I thank You for Your sacrificial death, burial, and resurrection of Your only begotten Son, our Lord Jesus Christ, who suffered, died, and was gloriously resurrected for our redemption.

I thank you for always being my strength, my refuge, and my fortress, One in whom I can always hide under the shelter of your wings. I cannot thank You enough for healing and delivering me from all my pain and sorrows. Your peace, joy, and strength have been my comfort through all the storms in life, and I cannot thank You enough.

I commit myself to You for Your service with the help of the Holy Spirit. Thank You for Your Word, which is a lamp to my feet and a light to my path.

Thank You, Heavenly Father, for the call and inspiration to author this book of healing and deliverance. I pray that my readers will be drawn to You and experience Your mighty healing and deliverance in their lives.

Thank You Holy Spirit. You have been my instructor, counselor, and guide through writing this book. Thank You for Your evident presence and anointing as I wrote under your direction.

To You, and You alone, I give all the glory, honor, and praise, in the mighty and precious name of your only begotten Son, the Lord Jesus Christ of Nazareth. Be exalted Mighty God!!!!
In the precious Name of Jesus, Amen

~Pearlene, Your "Precious Pearl"

Special Thanks

Special thanks to my husband Tom for his love, patience, and encouragement as I took time away from him to spend with the Lord and to write this book. To my beloved children Chris, Steph, Nick, and Jon, who kept saying, "Mummy, take time to write what God has given to you. Pull your journals out and write."

To my sisters and Prayer Partners of God's Precious Pearls Ministry, thank you for your love, prayers, encouragement and financial support in producing God's work, as we work together in His name. I cannot thank you enough for all your fervent and continued prayers and your listening ears. This meant a lot to me, and may the Lord forever bless you.

My Sister Pat Livingston, who was a great source of strength and encouragement through her prayers, many weekly calls on the progress of *Broken into Wholeness*. "Keep going sis, but don't forget to rest."

Without the love, kindness, and attentive care of special people in my life during the difficult time I faced, I would not have made it this far. Special mention to Mr. and Mrs. Lloyd Jenkins, Dr. and the late Mrs. Keith Davidson, Mrs. Winsome Davies and the late Tony Davies, Dr. and Mrs. Daryll (Daz) Twigger, Mr. and Mrs. Godfrey Batson. You were all a source of great strength and encouragement to me. I cannot thank you enough. You stood with me, dried my tears and comforted me when I felt all hope was lost.

Special thanks to my "spiritual midwife," Sister in the Lord, and friend of over forty years Apostle Tamara Blow Ed.D., RN, who helped to birth the writing of this book through her encouragement. Thank you for taking the time to proofread my manuscripts before publishing and for your professional input.

To my special niece, Dr. Kamilah Jackson MD, MPH, Child, and Adolescent Psychiatry Specialist, who encouraged me all the way to complete this book, as "this is so needed today, Auntie." Thank you, Kam, for your listening ear and your inspiration.

To my spiritual daughter Naana, who encouraged and blessed me with the many different teas, my favorite teas from England to sip on, and the many tasty goodies to munch on while I write.

Last but not least, I do not have enough words to say thank you to my very special spiritual daughter, Jacinth Headlam. Jac, you have been and continue to be my writing mentor, editor, director, encourager, and motivator with our weekly Zoom meetings throughout the trimesters of birthing this book. You are a Godsend at this time of my life, where He is using you to bring forth what He has instructed me to do in the golden years of my life. Honestly, without you, I would not have been able to do this, through His grace. May God continue to bless your vision of InnaStar Ministry in the Arts and all that you put your hands to do. You are so well-versed in what you do with excellence, wisdom, knowledge, and understanding.

PEARLENE FRIDAY

Love you always,
Pearlene / Mama Pearl ♡

About the Author

Pearlene, the second of five children, was raised in a Christian home in Jamaica, West Indies by loving parents who nurtured her in the ways of the Lord. She was born again at an early age and received the baptism of the Holy Spirit in 1987.

Trained and educated as a registered nurse and midwife in Essex, England, she was recruited from London, by the Medical College of Virginia University Hospital, where she worked for many years. Three months after arriving in the United States, she met her husband, Tom. They have been happily married for 40 years and are the blessed parents of four married children which includes three sons (Christopher, Nicholas, and Jonathan), one daughter (Stephanie), three lovely grandsons (Thomas, Benjamin, and Fitzgerald), two precious granddaughters (Veda and Josephine), and a blessed step-grandson (Joshua). They are all Nana's heart and joy.

Pearlene loves the Lord and enjoys reading and studying His Word, and she is learning daily to be still to listen to His gentle voice. She enjoys wonderful times of prayer and fellowship with Him. She is a prophetic intercessor, a licensed and ordained minister of the Gospel, and a chaplain.

Having pursued studies in pastoral care, she has worked as a chaplain within the hospital. She is the founder of "God's Precious Pearls" ministry, where she enjoys mentoring and teaching the Word of God, as well as encouraging and mentoring God's daughters from her life's experience, according to Titus 2. She is "Mama Pearl" to many young women and "Nana Pearl" to her precious grandchildren.

For relaxation she enjoys sewing, cooking, decorating her home, gardening, and writing. She places much emphasis in making her home a "Haven of Rest" for her family and all who enter, where they can experience an atmosphere of God's peace and His love. She feels the body of Christ needs to be encouraged and strengthened daily.

A couple of guiding scriptures that she lives by are, "Therefore encourage one another and build each other up, just in fact as you are doing" (1 Thess. 1:11) NIV and "But encourage one another daily, as long as it is called today, so that none of you will be hardened by sin's deceitfulness" (Hebrews 3:13 KJV). Especially during these crucial days we are living in, it is important to know that the battle increases but surely the victory is ours.

She strives to walk daily with the Holy Spirit and trust Him to lead her each day in the blueprint of her life, which was ordained before she was knitted in her mother's womb. (See Psalm 139:14-16 KJV).

For further information on the ministry of encouragement and exhortation through God's Precious Pearls Ministry, you may contact her at God's Precious Pearls Ministry Gems123@ptd.net .

Pearlene Friday is the Founder and Director of
God's Precious Pearls Ministry.

GodsPreciouspPearls.blogspot.com
GodsPreciousPearls facebook
GodsPreciousPearls facebook group

www.ingramcontent.com/pod-product-compliance
Lightning Source LLC
Chambersburg PA
CBHW061159120626
46546CB00005B/2120